Syl
19(
Poems

Eva Mendelsson – Martin Ruch (Publ.)
Translation Marion Godfrey

Sylvia Cohn (1904–1942)
Poems and letters

Anthology on the occasion of the centenary
of the birthday of the Offenburg-born writer
and poet 5 May 2004
with contribution by Ursula Flügler

Frontpicture: Sylvia Cohn in the French camp at Rivesaltes. The last photo, 1941

Eva Mendelsson (England), youngest daughter of Sylvia Cohn. In October 1940, at the age of 9, Eva was deported to Gurs concentration camp in France with her mother and sister. From there, the two children were rescued and escaped to Switzerland.

Ursula Flügler (Offenburg), Latin and German teacher till 2002. 1978 book of poems "Erstes Lateinbuch". Collaboration on books, publications in journals.

Martin Ruch (Offenburg), freelance publicist on regional and cultural history topics, including the history of Offenburg's Jews.

Marion Godfrey, translator, London, daughter of German refugees, Civilisation Française and Philosophy graduate, has translated many books in a long career in translation and interpreting.

© KulturAgentur Dr. Martin Ruch
Gestaltung: punktgenau GmbH, Bühl
Herstellung und Verlag: BoD – Books on Demand, Norderstedt, 2022
Printed in Germany
ISBN-13: 978-3-7557-9114-0

Content

Foreword by Eva Mendelsson 7

Introduction 8

Biography 11

On the poems of Sylvia Cohn 26

Early poems 1919–1933 33

Poems 1933–1940 65

Poems 1940–42 101

Selected letters 121

Plays 138

Bibliography 159

Foreword by Eva Mendelsson

Dearest Mother,
Who would have thought that when I asked you for a few poems you had written for my eleventh birthday, these would become my greatest treasure and companions for life! It makes me so happy that through the poems you have left me, you will live forever in my heart.

I was a little girl of eight when our family was torn apart, and I could not then understand what consequences this would have for our lives.

I have come to know you through all that you have written. Your lines sing out with your love for us children and for father, for nature, the birds, also your longing, your suffering and above all, your love for the Black Forest, for home.

It is important to me that anyone who reads this book will see that that you had not a shred of hate in you and that you were always true to your religion in your short life.

Your daughter Eva, also on behalf of your other daughters, Esther and Myriam.

It has always been my dearest wish that my mother's short life would be crowned by the publication of her poems. I feel a profound sense of satisfaction that this is now a reality and that through this book, my mother and her memory will live on.

Introduction

"A rosy glow in the firmament portends an end to the suffering" The lyrical work of the Offenburg writer Sylvia Cohn ends in March 1942 with this strong image of hope. In another poem at the time, she had written "No, our God does not forget us", showing the strength she drew from her faith. The spectrum of her poems is clear evidence that this faith had grown even stronger since 1933. However the hope to an end of the horror is in vain and on 30 September 1942, Sylvia Cohn died in Auschwitz of "a sudden heart attack". The death certificate signed by concentration camp doctor, Johann Kremer, is patently untrue: Sylvia did not die of natural causes.. "A rosy glow in the firmament" – this image of hope was not fulfilled for Sylvia Cohn.

In the Rivesaltes camp in the south of France, Sylvia took courage once again. Even two years after the brutal deportation from Offenburg, she was determined not to give up, despite the depression and despair all around. "Be strong in my heart and have patience" was another appeal from Sylvia, who by now was suffering from heart disease and asthma. The two children, Eva and Myriam, who had been deported with her, were sent to live in a French children's home, where they were able to attend school, and that at least was some small consolation. Eldest daughter, Esther, had stayed in Munich and found a good home in the Antonienstrasse. Sylvia only rarely had news of her, but she was reassured. Occasionally, letters were still being sent from England, where her husband Eduard had been able to emigrate and was trying to bring over his family as quickly as possible. However, the outbreak of war in 1939 had frustrated these plans. Sylvia was alone and suffering: "I am a prisoner and alone." Almost all the necessary papers for leaving via Portugal were available in Rivesaltes, just one document was still missing …

Sylvia Cohn had been writing poems and other lyrical works since she was very young. What remains of these is in the possession of her youngest daughter, Eva. The collection, which also includes letters, is very extensive. For the present anthology, the works giving voice to the poet's essential themes have been selected from this comprehensive body of work.

Our intention as editors was to return a Jewish poet and her work to the city of Offenburg. Especially in the years from about 1930 onwards, the lyrical expressiveness and powerful imagery of the texts is striking. These poems and letters document the life of a Jewish woman from the state of Baden in Germany and reflect her life with the family and her life in the community and the state under increasingly horrific and brutal conditions. A whole life is presented here in lyric poetry in its private and its political-public perspectives. It is a unique work and is important as a poetic as well as a contemporary historical document.

A further motivation for publication of these poems was prompted by a request from deceased philosopher and rabbi, Emil Fackenheim. Born in Halle in 1916, he was able to escape the Holocaust to Scotland and died in Jerusalem in 2003. The German weekly magazine "Die Zeit" calls him "the most important Jewish thinker of the present". Emil Fackenheim added a 614th to the 613 mitzvot (commandments in the Jewish faith): Hitler should under no circumstances be rewarded with a retrospective victory, and that all evidence, traces and testimonies of those murdered must be collected and preserved in order to save them from total extermination. In this vein, Sylvia Cohn's poems will now also be collected and preserved for the future. Her voice was not silenced in Auschwitz. Hitler did not win.

Martin Ruch

Biography

The Jewish community of Offenburg had reached its peak with about 500 members around 1900, since when their number had been steadily declining. When the Nazis came to power, Offenburg still had about 300 Jews, of whom a hundred had been murdered by 1945. The others managed to escape. By 1945, there was no longer a Jewish community in Offenburg.

Sylvia Oberbrunner, 1916

Sylvia Oberbrunner was born in Offenburg on 5 May 1904. Her father, Eduard Elias Oberbunner (1860–1932) was a wine wholesaler and distiller of spirits. As a respected citizen and local councillor, he was also active in the young Jewish community (in 1862 the complete civic equality of those of Israelitic faith had become law in the State of Baden) as an officer of the synagogue and long-term chairman of the synagogue. He was married to Emma Kahn (1865–1922), whose father Moritz Kahn was also a wine merchant and Eduard Oberbrunner subsequently took over his father in law's business.

The couple had five daughters: Irma (1886, married Wetzlar), Brunhilde (1887, married Lipper), Elise (1888, married Wetzlar), Martha (1890), and as a late child, Sylvia (1904, married Cohn).

Sylvia wrote her first poems while she was still at school in Offenburg. The family had its business premises and a flat at Wilhelmstraße 15. Her parents and a large circle of friends, including her teacher, Professor Stärk, encouraged her in her writing. Sylvia remained on friendly terms in contact with the professor and his family for many years. Some letters bear witness to this. For example, in 1918, the teacher wrote: "My dear student, I thank you very much for the beautiful lines that brought me great joy: I look forward to working with you soon." Perhaps that was when Sylvia had sent her revered professor her lyrical fairy tale: "What the lily told the myrtle tree in the quiet place" and in fact, she had dedicated the poem to him. Other youthful lyrical fairy tales are a "A birthday tale" and "Children and flowers". The magic of innocence permeates this enchanted world of childhood and youth.

In December 1924, Eduard Oberbrunner announced the engagement of his youngest daughter Sylvia to the merchant Eduard Cohn (1898–1976) from Schönsee in West Prussia. The son-in-law was to take over the Oberbrunner wine trading company one day. The marriage took place the following year on the bride's 21st birthday (5 May 1925). The young couple honeymooned in Italy and in her

Wedding of Sylvia Oberbrunner and Eduard Cohn, 1925

poem "Chianti", Sylvia described this romantic journey. It is a happy time, as she confesses to her husband on 3 September, four months after the wedding: "Oh, my darling, there is so much beauty on this earth all around us and in us. For all that lives, all that is here, is a part of His great, all-encompassing divine love and only when we begin to experience it in ourselves, can we better understand the purpose of life".

The family grew with the arrival of children and in this next generation too, the young parents have only girls: Esther (1926–1944), Myriam (1929–1975) and Eva (1931). Perhaps the last birth in March 1931 weakened Sylvia and August finds her as a patient in the Freiburg gynaecological clinic. There she received a letter from her mother's friend, Mrs. Stärk, saying: "… that you have survived the difficult days well and are restored to full health. Yesterday evening, I waited at your home for your husband's telephone call

Sylvia's contribution to her school's 50th anniversary celebrations

and it was delightful to see how the little ones were interested in how their mother was doing. Esther even wanted to know what you had for dinner ...!"

In all other respects, unfortunately, daily life in Offenburg was becoming increasingly dominated by business worries. Although Eduard was busy as a salesman travelling all over Germany, in his letters to his family, the sentence "Good health when business is bad ..." appeared more and more frequently, and less and less frequently, he wrote: "Business was good today, after rain comes sunshine." The shortage of money was also mentioned, for instance, on his birthday in 1932, when he had to be away from home on a trip once again. By way of exception, Eduard says he will call Offenburg, but under no circumstances should Sylvia buy him anything, because: "If you spend money, I'll get angry and won't call!"

Eduard wrote regularly when he was on the road and participated in family life as a loving father. In January 1926, he wrote from Donaueschingen: "Darling, I'll drink a toast with you and drink to your health and to us!" And he went on to remind Sylvia of their honeymoon trip to Laurana, saying: "... we should celebrate those memories, look back over those wonderful times and hope for even more wonderful times in the future!"

In June 1934, he wrote anxiously from the Hotel Luisenhof in Hanover: "So, you poor devils, all of you are hurt? You should be more careful. How can anyone fall out of a hammock? Have you ever seen the rope break when I lie in it? Or have you been swinging in it?"

He never forgot the children in his letters and all of them received loving cards, sometimes one to all three addressed to: "The home of the 3 Cohn girls, Wilhelmstrasse 15."

Occasional breaks in the Black Forest show us that Sylvia sometimes found the burden of the children and the household difficult. Maybe this is why she stayed in Uehlingen (Black Forest) in 1930. The poems written at that time show us that she is anxious. In the poem "Gebet – A Prayer" she writes as early as January 1928 that she is "plagued by melancholy" and in 1939, she writes of her "sorrowful soul" in a letter to her sister Hilde. Her friend Gertrud Moritz tries to cheer her up: "You have a good husband and two dear children who need you. A mother should never be anxious or desperate."

Poem created on the occasion of a concert circa 1930

In 1931, the parents are hit hard: their eldest daughter Esther falls ill with polio. For months, she lies in hospital in Karlsruhe. She survives, but the consequences of the disease are irreversible and as a result, Esther will subsequently have to wear leg callipers.

Poems and letters 1933–1940: we share a common burden

"No, it is not beautiful here under the sign of the swastika, as you can imagine. Where do we go from here? No, I can tell you, it feels very much like the "calm before the storm" ...and there have already been a few rumblings of an imminent thunderstorm," she wrote to Gertrud Moritz on 1 March 1933.

The poems that are now being written clearly show the traces of these first forebodings of the thunderstorm to come. At the beginning of that fateful year, 1933, an immediate preoccupation with Jewish themes sets in. Sylvia's poems are now defined by outrage at the National Socialists' racial pollicies on the one hand and solidarity and hope for emigration on the other. Infuriated, she registered, for example, the increasing discrimination of the Jewish soldiers who had fought for the Kaiser and the Reich in the First World War: "Is this why you went through the war, so that people would make fun of your nose today? As early as September 1933, she speaks of Eretz Israel as the true home of all Jews: "Take us in, do not reject us!" Yet it is difficult for her to let go of her love for her German homeland, the Black Forest.

Since Jewish artists were denied access to cultural establishments and organisations from 1933 onwards, they founded a nationwide Kulturbund Deutscher Juden – the German Jewish Cultural Association. By 1935, there were more than 36 regional or local cultural associations with about 70,000 members in 100 towns and cities. Artists, actors and painters, poets and craftsmen, singers and musicians performed in Jewish cultural centres and synagogues and ensured an active cultural life. Sylvia Cohn was also involved in the Kulturbund and she participated in a competition in March 1935 with her stage play "Esther" (also performed in Offenburg), which was well received.[1]

---

[1] Participating authors and the plays they submitted: "They were Fritz Rosenthal of Munich (Das Messiasspiel); Maurice Ruebner (Pax eterna) and Oswald Pander (Man türmt), both of Ham-

Sylvia was becoming increasingly involved in social work for the Offenburg congregation: "On Sunday, 17 January 1937, at 9 o'clock in the morning, the congregation council was called to a meeting. (…) On the same day, at 3 o'clock, the general assembly of the Israelitic Women's Association took place in the synagogue hall. (…) Mrs. Neu was elected as the first chairwoman and secretary. Mrs Sylvia Cohn, Paula Kahn and Irene Lederer were newly elected to the Board. After the general assembly, we enjoyed a congenial get-together over coffee and cake."[2]

She wrote pieces for synagogue events, performing some of them herself, as the following minutes testify: "At 8 o'clock in the evening of 24 January 1937, members of the congregation were invited to a lecture in the synagogue hall. Our local writer, Mrs. Sylvia Cohn, read from her own poems, entitled "Of yesterday and today". These are poems about her experiences in the landscape, about home and love, as well as poems set in the context of the times. The third part of the performance, "Ahasver" – Ahazuerus – a stage play in 10 scenes, resonated particularly well and received enthusiastic applause from the audience. Teacher Bär, who opened the evening with a welcome address, was able to close the proceedings with praise and thanks to the author, Mrs Cohn."[3]

---

burg; Herbert Schoenlank of Amsterdam (Kalenner fahren Auto); Martin Mansbacher of Luebeck (Hanukkafestspiel); and Sylvia Cohn-Oberbrunner of Offenburg/Baden (Esther)". "Our competition! The decision of the jury", in: Mitteilungsblätter des Jüdischen Kulturbundes Rhein-Ruhr, March 1935, 7th quote after: Duewell,K.: Jewish Cultural Centres in Nazi Germany. Expectations and Accomplishments, in: J. Reinharz & W. Schatzberg (eds.), The Jewish Response to German Culture, From the Enlightenment to the Second World War. Hanover-London, 1985, 294–316.

[2] Israelitisches Gemeindeblatt Karlsruhe, 24.2.1937, p. 9
[3] Israelitisches Gemeindeblatt Karlsruhe, 24.2.1937, p. 9

At this time, Eduard Cohn was chairman of the local Zionist group in Offenburg. Sylvia also felt increasingly attracted to Zionism, which is probably why she was the sole representative of the Offenburg group to attend the 20th Zionist Congress in Zurich. On August 9 1937, Sylvia sent a card from the Hotel Bellerive au Lac in Zurich to her husband: "To the Board of the Z.O.G. Zionist group) Offenburg ... Dear Ed" However, she writes somewhat enigmatically: "This is the miracle of Loch Ness. / In truth I wasn't attending a congress, / this card my thoughts are defining / as I sit here incognito dining. / When I come home I will have much to say / Of the dramatic events and interesting word play! Warmest kisses, Yours, Sylvia."

She found moving words for everyday life under the oppressive special laws of the Nazis in the poem "Frühling 1938 für Großstadtjuden" – Spring 1938 for city Jews: "They still pretend it is yesterday / Play with the dog, go for coffee today / All my brothers and sisters of the same strain / Sharing a common burden of pain.

Vocabulary notebook: Sylvia Cohn was learning Hebrew in preparation for emigration

In the early morning of 10 November 1938, the night of "Reichskristallnacht" or crystal night, a name too pretty for the terrible events of that night, Eduard Cohn was arrested and taken to prison with the other male Jews of Offenburg. That evening, on the way to the railway station, they had to walk past a screaming horde of onlookers and party-goers before arriving at the station, where they were taunted and beaten. A train took them to Dachau, where the humiliations and torture continued. The first reports of a fatality soon reached Offenburg: Jakob Adler (1867–1938) died under torture. After a few weeks, the prisoners were released but only on condition that they would remain silent about their stay in the concentration camp and leave Germany as quickly as possible. Eduard Cohn returned from Dachau to Offenburg on 20 December 1938, just in time to celebrate Chanukah – the Jewish festival of lights commemorating the miracle of the oil in the eternal light of the Temple, which, although only enough for one day, lasted for eight days until a runner could bring more oil. Much relieved, it was a happy reunion for the whole family. At the same time, the final decision to emigrate was made.

In May 1939, Eduard Cohn travelled ahead to England to make preparations for the emigration of the whole

Munich 1939: Family photo taken for their father: Esther, Eva, Myriam (l to r)

family. However, the outbreak of war in September 1939 thwarted his plans and emigration was no longer a possibility.

When war broke out, due to the proximity of the French border, Sylvia Cohn and her children escaped to safety in Munich, where she found shelter and help from Jewish women ("A little woman with a warm heart, an alert mind and understanding, giving a sisterly hand to a woman in need and pain"), but returns with the two youngest girls after a few months when the danger had appeared to pass. Esther remained in the Munich children's home, where she was able to complete her high school education. As top of the class, she was allowed to give the valedictory speech, closing with the words of the psalm, Isaiah 40:31: "But those who hope in the Lord will renew their strength. They will soar on wings like eagles; they will run and not grow weary, they will walk and not be faint ...".

In 1942 she was deported to Theresienstadt and finally murdered in Auschwitz in October 1944, two years after the death of her mother.

Poems and letters 22.10.1940–30.9.1942: It's murder, I tell you

On 22 October 1940, some 6,500 Jews from the Baden-Palatinate were deported to France. One hundred Jews from Offenburg, including Sylvia Cohn, were rounded up in the gymnasium of the Oberrealschule high school (now the Schillergymnasium), where they remained until their deportation in the evening. They had to sign a waiver of their property and were only allowed to take the barest essentials with them. The purpose of the deportation is unclear at first. Many fear a trip to the east. But when the bridge over the Rhine near Breisach is crossed in the direction of

Colmar, everyone began to breathe a little easier, because they believed that France would be the lesser evil. Perhaps they might even have hoped they could reach freedom from there. However, they soon discovered that the conditions in the Gurs camp in Southern France were horrific. In the first winter, 1,050 people died from the cold, illness and malnutrition. In 1941, some were able to escape the camp to find shelter outside. Sylvia Cohn was not given the opportunity to do so, but at least her two daughters were accommodated in a children's home, where they could also attend school. On 16 March 1941, Sylvia was resettled in the "hospital camp" at Rivesaltes, by the Mediterranean sea.

January 1942 saw the Wannsee conference organised, rather than resolved, the murder, since that issue had already been decided beforehand. The French Vichy government collaborated with the Nazis, working with these criminals to allow the deportation of German Jews from the South of France back to Germany and on to Poland.

By the time she had reached the camps at Gurs and Rivesaltes, Sylvia Cohn was already heartbroken. She also suffered from asthma and needed daily medication, which she carried in her suitcase. However, in the confusion, there was a mix-up between this suitcase and her daughter Myriam's when she was transported to Auschwitz, and as a result, Myriam would suffer greatly from this all her life, feeling partly to blame for the death of her beloved mother. Myriam's memory of this event was particularly painful when she herself turned 38, the age at which her mother had died.

Sylvia had a picture taken for the children one last time and enclosed it in her letter of 9 December 1941 to Eva and Myriam, who were in the children's home at the time. Eva Mendelsson remembered this picture when putting together the anthology of poetry and letters 1992: "The dress was green and on it was a silver brooch. Mother had wavy hair. In the background are rubble, dirt and the wasteland that was Rivesaltes. All we could see was barbed wire and the terrible latrines. It's the very last picture we have of her."

Eva takes up the story: "On 1 September 1942 we were taken back to the camp. This time, we knew that we were going to Auschwitz with mother. I was glad to see my mother again. It never occurred to me that this would be our final farewell. I was eleven years old and Myriam 13, and since we were under 14, mother was given the option of leaving us behind in the camp at Rivesaltes, which she chose to do on the promise that they would do everything to keep us alive. On 13 September 1942, mother's transport left. She was 38 years old. I cannot describe the look on my mother's face as she was taken away and separated from us, as we stood behind the barbed wir fence." Sylvia Cohn's only consolation in the great misfortune will have been the thought that her children would be safe. The French children's aid organisation OSE (Oeuvres secours aux enfants) was able to save many children.

Sylvia Cohn in the French camp at Rivesaltes. The last photo, 1941

Swiss nurse, Friedel Bohny-Reiter, worked in the Rivesaltes camp during those months. In her diary, she describes the deportations, including those of 13 September 1942: "It's half past one. We've just come back from the station. We were down there from 3 o'clock in the afternoon. Today was truly terrible. There were already scenes in the barracks, with some fainting. From 7 am to 11 am, the people were standing outside at roll call in the blazing hot sun. I can still hear the screaming of the women. I could still manage to take the children from one of the mothers, but as I went to take them away, she grasped them tightly in her arms. I released the children from her embrace and took them back inside. The woman refused to get into the truck, so the guards picked her up and lifted her into it."[4]

From Rivesaltes, the transport first headed north to the Le Bourget – Drancy transit camp (north of Paris). Three days later, on 16 September, at 8.55 a.m., railway convoy No. 33 left for Auschwitz. 586 men and 407 women, including Sylvia Cohn, were crammed into the cattle trucks.[5] The record of events at Auschwitz – Birkenau Concentration Camp noted the arrival on 18 September 1942 of the train: "With the 33rd transport of the Reich Security Main Office from France, 1,003 Jewish men, women and children have arrived. A first selection, in which probably 300 men were transferred to various labour camps, took place in Cosel. After the selection in Auschwitz, 147 women, who were given the numbers 19980 to 20216, were admitted to the camp as prisoners: "Extermination through labour" is their

---

[4] Bohny-Reiter, Friedel: Vorhof der Vernichtung. Diary of a Swiss sister in the French internment camp Rivesaltes 1941–1942. Konstanz 1995, 119

[5] Completed form of Diane Afoumado, Centre de Documentation Juive Contemporaine, Paris, by mail of 12.12.2003

lot. The remaining 556 deportees were immediately taken to the gas chambers and killed."[6]

Sylvia Cohn lived for another 12 days as a registered prisoner in Auschwitz. After that, the SS camp doctor, Johann Kremer[7], issued a death certificate noting: cause of death at 1:45 a.m. on 30 September 1942 of Sylvia Cohn: sudden heart attack, although it is only too certain that Sylvia did not die of natural causes and that this statement by the concentration camp doctor is a complete lie.[8]

---

[6] Czech, Danuta: Kalendarium der Ereignisse im Konzentrationslager [Calendar of events at the concentration camp] Auschwitz-Birkenau 1939-1945. Reinbek bei Hamburg. 1989, P. 304.

[7] Johann Kremer (1883-1965), anatomist and SS doctor, was in Auschwitz-Birkenau from 29.8. to 18.11.1942 as a deputy in Auschwitz. He selected people for the gas chambers at the ramp and carried out experiments on hunger research. Noted in his diary on 23.9.1942: "Dinner with Obergruppenführer Pohl in the evening at 8 p.m. in the Führer home, a real feast. There was roast pike, as much as everyone wanted, real coffee, excellent beer and sandwiches." On 10.10.1942: „Living fresh material of liver, spleen and pancreas taken and fixed." Sentenced to death by Supreme Polish People's Tribunal Krakow on 22.12.1947, commuted to life on the grounds of age, released in Poland in 1958. Sentenced to ten years imprisonment by the Münster Regional Court on 29.11.1960 but deemed to have served this during the Polish imprisonment. From: Klee, Ernst: Das Personenlexikon zum Dritten Reich. {Who's who in the third reich] Frankfurt 2003, p. 338 f

[8] Death certificate 33667/1942 of 6.10.1942 (photocopy archive museum Auschwitz; documented in: Staatliches Museum Auschwitz-Birkenau (eds.): Death records of Auschwitz, vol. 2, Munich 1995, 184). – Letter from the director Jerzy Wroblewski, Museum Auschwitz, 8.4.1995, to Ursula Flügler: "However, the cause of death and the time of death did not always correspond to the truth. The military hospitals wrote in the death certificates as the cause of death one of the illnesses that could be taken from an official list issued by the camp doctor. In order to cover up mass executions, the names of the murdered people were often gradu-

Biography

```
Nr. 33667/1942  (643)                    [STAMP: AUSCHWITZ]        C¹

                              Auschwitz, den 6. Oktober      19 42

      Die Sylvia Cohn geborene Oberbrunner

                                           mosaisch
wohnhaft  Offenburg in Baden, Friedenstrasse Nr. 46

ist am  3o. September 1942      um  o1  Uhr  45  Minuten

in  Auschitz, Kasernenstrasse                      verstorben.

      Die Verstorbene war geboren am  5. Mai 19o4

In  Offenburg

(Standesamt                                   Nr.         )

Vater:  Eduard Oberbrunner, zuletzt wohnhaft in Offenburg


Mutter:  Emma Oberbrunner geborene Kahn, zuletzt wohnhaft
in Hirsau

Die Verstorbene war — nicht — verheiratet  mit Eduard Cohn


Eingetragen auf mündliche — schriftliche Anzeige  des Arztes Doktor der
Medizin Kremer in Auschwitz vom 3o. September 1942



                                Vorgelesen, genehmigt und       unterschrieben.

Die Übereinstimmung mit dem
Erstbuch wird beglaubigt.

Auschwitz, den 6. 10.  1942
                                      Der Standesbeamte
      Der Standesbeamte               In Vertretung
      In Vertretung                   Quakernack

Todesursache:  Plötzlicher Herztod


Eheschliessung de  Verstorbenen am         in
(Standesamt                                 Nr.         ).
```

Sylvia Cohn's death certificate: Source: Auschwitz archives

Martin Ruch

---

ally removed from the camp register with forged death certificates over several days. (Translator)

On the poems of Sylvia Cohn

"Gold rusts and steel decays,
Marble crumbles, death comes to all in the end
Grief is the most permanent of earthly emotions.
But longest lasting is the Divine word."

A quiet calmness borne of certainty characterises the mood of this poem by the Russian poet Anna Achmatowa, which she wrote in 1945 – the Russians also having experienced the horrors of the century and its disasters. The words of the poets can survive destruction and what is collected here in this book is saved from destruction. It has survived and can bear witness.

These poems, entrusted to flimsy paper, were light luggage. Sylvia Cohn's children, Myriam and Eva, took their mother's poems with them as a last memento of her on their flight to safety in Switzerland and have faithfully preserved them. What was left behind in Offenburg, when the family's last home was abandoned to looting after deportation to Gurs, was saved by their Catholic maid, Hermine Keller and at the end of the war in 1945, she was able to give Eduard Cohn the photos, letters and above all, the poems by his wife Sylvia.

This book contains only a selection of these works. Almost all of them are handwritten texts, some of them carefully written in books on good quality paper, the kind used for poetry anthologies and diaries. A conscious sense of purpose is evident in the collection, perhaps also the hope for publication. The poems written later in the Gurs camp are easily recognised by the meagerness of their appearance. Every scrap of paper was treasured and every format and space needed saving. Woollen threads, precious at this time of material hardship, staple the small sheets together with poems that Sylvia Cohn wrote down, partly from memory. How far-sighted of Eva as a child, because these poems became "a treasure and a companion for life" of the motherless young girl.

It has now been more than twenty years since I first came across copies of these poems written in German script in Gurs, with their scrappy appearance and their moving message. The more I became acquainted with Sylvia Cohn's poems over the years, the more I felt that they were indeed a legacy. The fact that they are now collected and printed seems to me as if I have finally fulfilled a duty.

Sylvia Cohn encountered poetry at an early age. The German middle classes were immensely proud of their poets. In fact, text books and German teachers regarded it as their task to inspire students to treasure the tradition of poetry … and learning by heart was a part of this process. It was certainly no torture for the language-gifted child, Sylvia. The later confidence with which Sylvia Cohn moved in the melodic forms and language patterns of the classical and romantic eras is probably due in part to her early encounter with the rhythm of verse and the melodiousness of rhyme. The joy of writing may also have developed early on from her initially playful attempts to reproduce the basic forms and patterns of verse.

The Jewish citizens of Offenburg did not live in the "schtetl" like the Jews of Eastern Europe. They felt at home in the German language and culture. Sylvia Cohn was allowed to attend the Mädchen-Oberrealschule high school, today's Okengymnasium grammar school. German language and culture were her home and her milieu, like her beloved Black Forest and the landscape of the Upper Rhine of which she was particularly fond. However, at least Sylvia's deportation to Gurs could not rob her of the language, her "mother tongue" (Rose Ausländer).

Sylvia's early poems illustrate with great clarity a sensitive young girl, full of anticipation, longing, and no small hint of apprehension. The different seasons, or 'moods' of Nature correspond to the moods of the soul – often in four line stanza form, echoing the folksongs of the German Romanticism of the late 18th and early 19th century. However, the realism of a prescient 'nevertheless' that reins in the ebb and flow of emotions and urges courage and patience is already evident in Sylvia's early poems. "Be strong, my heart, and have patience" – even in Gurs, the exhausted heart is still admonished to hope.

Feelings are often characterised by ambivalence. For example, in the Meersburg poem, there is a sense of foreboding underlying the happiness:

"Leaning against the ancient monastery wall, I turn
And looking down deep in thought I yearn
Seeing that boundless sweet sorrow ...
I see happiness and a grave ... and await tomorrow".

However, at this time, Sylvia is preoccupied with the fundamental issues of womanhood: love, betrothal, marriage and motherhood. Perhaps her 1927 poem, "First Flight," uses the metaphor of flight to show very clearly the nature of her plan for life and her desire for happiness:

"Descent is cruel, but ascent is a joy!
Gaze now directed far beyond the empty horizon ...
Secure in the knowledge of existence of other
Soaring upwards in full flight!"

Later poems reflect the descent into depression. The disappointment of everyday married life, the struggle for material existence, Esther's polio and almost simultaneously, the birth of her third child, Eva, caused Sylvia to fall into severe despondency, almost despair, in 1930/31. There are many poems from this time. They are written in the hospital and during her convalescence. Such times were an opportunity for Sylvia, as the mother of three small children, who did not really have her own space at home, to recover her senses and write. Running through the poems like a thread is the consoling balm of "the solitude of the universe", of Nature:

*"... and out of the narrowness of my existence
breaks forth an irrepressible joy."*

Until about 1930, it would be hard to deduce from the poems that Sylvia Cohn was Jewish in a Jewish community, so unquestionably secure her life seems to have been before that time. However, the events after 1933 changed her perceptions and consequently, the tone of her poems. A poem on New Year's Eve 1930 concluded with a portentious:

*"If we knew what lay ahead,
Our suffering would be the greater."*

On the occasion of the boycott of Jewish shops, on 4 April 1933, the "Jüdische Rundschau" newspaper urged Jews to: "Wear it with pride, the yellow spot! , meaning the compulsory yellow star, which, at this stage, was still only a metaphor for discrimination. Sylvia Cohn had certainly read the newspaper article, and many poems reflect her engagement with the topic of growing persecution:

*"Shall I now wear the yellow spot,
Just because "I'm a Jew"?*

Bitter is the experience of being forced to be a stranger in one's own home:

"Must be Jewish, must be different …"

Self-awareness and sadness ring out from the lines:

*"The German spirit has espoused
The culture you call Jewish;
It tortured Heine still to find
A Jewish soul within him"*

The lines allude to Heinrich Heine, who, despite having himself baptised, could never quite let go of his Jewishness.

From here on, Sylvia identified passionately with Jewish destiny. She made a conscious effort to work with the Jewish community and there are many testimonies of her practical and spiritual abilities, which she developed in the service of the community. In particular, her play "Ahasver – Ahasuerus [Xerxes]" shows how thoroughly Sylvia reflected on the role Jews played in the course of history – and how she visualised these connections in the language of poetry. Ahasver, or Xerxes, endlessly wandering, is finally allowed to die because he knows that his people have arrived in "Eretz Israel":

*"That my old eyes can still bear witness …
and see our people rebuilding our land,
our ancient homeland, bride of the heart …"*

Eduard Cohn had also intended to emigrate to Israel with his family. For Eduard, it would have meant salvation, but for the poetess Sylvia Cohn, it would also have meant linguistic exile. A particularly impressive poem was written in the Gurs camp. It describes in epic breadth and in long, dense sentences, the odyssey of the transport and the misery of the Gurs camp. It contains a painful memory of 20 December 1938: the return of her husband from Dachau in time to celebrate Chanukah. She had meanwhile been deported to Gurs without her husband, who was preparing the family's emigration in England, and this magnified her misery and the feeling of being completely alone and abandoned. The image of the broken ship of life, drifting rudderless without a mast, appears several times in the poems. There are poems in which she, a pious woman, also sees herself abandoned by God. Only with difficulty does she master the temptation to reject her faith:

"Almighty Father, hear my cries
When, Oh when will You set us free?
When will You hear our fervent pleas?
A festival! The melodies, ancient and familiar
Rise up to heaven in supplication and yet
We cannot see God."

In her poems, she explicitly gives evil a name: Hitler and his crimes. In one of her poems, recalling Cassandra, her voice warns: *"I'm telling you, it's murder!"*

The poems written in Gurs and Rivesaltes express the truth in the language of poetry – a truth that speaks for itself in tandem with the irrefutable evidence of hard fact and documentary records. The language and the way in which the letters were written reveal to us the circumstances under which the poems were written. Life in the camp was a daily struggle simply to survive, to try and obtain exit papers and to rescue the children. The letters must be read in order to fully appreciate the extent of the material and emotional distress, and the pervasive fear inhabiting the young poetess at the time. Unlike the early poems, which depict the life of a gifted young woman in the vehicle of poetry, these are works that have become an existential necessity to survive mentally and spiritually in the sheer hell of the claustrophobia, filth and degradation of life in the camps. Yet at the same time, in their eloquence these poems testify to the powerlessness, the helplessness of the situation. They bear witness to what happened and to the suffering endured in a way that others not endowed with Sylvia Cohn's gift with words could not express. The poet Rose Ausländer survived the ghetto in Czernowitz. She later said for her: "Writing was life, survival."

For Sylvia Cohn, there was no survival. She was murdered in Auschwitz. This life, active, creative, maternal, was brutally ended at 38 years of age. However, although Sylvia herself died, that was not the end. We know who she was. She lives on through her poems.

Ursula Flügler

Early poems
1919–1933

Come, give me your hand

ONE MORNING
(1919)

Fragrant dawn, the summer skies
Silent, gentle breezes sweeping
Over my sore and reddened eyes
Burning from all the weeping.

Slowly the veil of mist o'er dales and hills
Is banished by another light
Every fibre of my being fills
With the wonder of creation's might.

Speaking, saying: what's the use of brooding
On the evils that our lives do blight?
Look around, stop your tears and musing
See – the glory of the world's still bright!

COME WITH ME
(February 1922, on seeing a painting)

Come, let us go, you and I, and pick flowers
Flowers whose beauty unfolds and surprises
Flowers whose loveliness defies an artist's powers
More glorious even than the Almighty devises
Come, a pretty posy let us make
Picking blooms so fresh and bright
To some passing stranger the posy we'll take
Whom the flowers will delight.

ON THE FIRST OF MAY 1921

The branches of young birch trees
Entwine to form an arch above my head
Am I dreaming of soft breezes,
Or am I still asleep in bed?

Arms full of fresh, young flowers
My beating heart is now at peace,
A blackbird is singing in some bower
Its song of yearning without cease.

There's a weeping deep within me
And yet joy runs light and free
Earth, come spread all Nature's splendour
And bathe us in your blessings tender.

AN EVENING STROLL
(1923)

When the moon shone yellow over the wheat field,
We took each other by the hand,
Those moments were so soft and special
As together we listened to the silence,
That heavy, pregnant silence.

How the wind moves the ripening grain,
The wheat bending low in humility,
Touching our souls and our senses,
As we watch, hearts filled with love …
Loving and lost in dreams.

How red the moon glows!
And the summer breeze sings its song,
Such a strange, sad sound,
It makes us happy – but also breeds an eerie fear
And as yet we still feel so at ease.

We are on the cusp of adulthood
Still in bud, but not far from maturity,
And we feel strong and engaged.
That's how the summer found us.

A NEW DAWN
(The day of betrothal 1925)

Give me your hand, you, and be silent,
Stay very, very still and quiet.
For now, because I will stay with you
A new dawn begins.

This new dawn shall be sweet and fine
And become pure and intimate.
Give me your hand, you, I am yours
Now we are one on this earth.

CHIANTI
(Honeymoon memories 1926)

You look into the vibrant ruby red wine,
And your soul carries you back
To the first time of our loving union,
To that rapturous, joyful happiness.

Seeing the sunlight, dancing and glowing,
The majestic splendour of the mountains
All this has kindled in our blood
The sweet fire that now envelopes us

The roar of the sea, the azure blue of the southern sky,
The pine trees quivering gently in the breeze –
Now you take the woman in your arms, your bride,
Forever after to be your "life's companion".

FOR ESTHER
(23 October 1926)

Do you hear the rain falling, my precious child?
Do you hear the autumn wind whistling wild?
Ah, you hear it, but you pay no heed,
Your smiling little face, so content as you sleep.

Wild and stormy the scudding clouds go
Wild and savage the stormy winds blow,
Wrenching remaining leaves from the trees,
And yet you smile in your dreams.

FIRST FLIGHT
(1927)

Descent is cruel, but ascent is a joy!
Gaze now directed far beyond the horizon ...
Chasing away the mist to open the distant vista
The spirit following the line of sight ...
Blue fragrant hills, luscious green meadows,
White reddish villages, rivers that flow
All this, the eyes gather in like fruit off the trees
Or is it just a dream?
Higher and higher, buzzing and humming
The engine surges, but where is the dread?
Higher with buzzing and whirring and humming,
Words fall silent in the roar of the wind,
Secure in the knowledge of existence of other
Soaring upwards in full flight flight!

HEGAU
(May 1927)

Blossoming landscape! Firmly spellbound
I gaze in wonder on your vastness profound
Delicate pink, now wearing your spring dress,
Devoted to all that you possess
To that fresh and beautiful new life –
Like a bride, your trees are in bloom, rife
With dreaming your spring dreams!

Golden meadows, fields of gold,
Lush green entwined in dark forests of old
Welcome! Lilac blooms of red and white,
Your beauty lingers in my sight as you
Hang in fragrant, heavy umbels
Cladding the ancient wall as it crumbles.

Soul, breathe, revel in your freedom,
Drink deep the peace of spring
that arrives clad in millions of blossoms.

AN AUTUMNAL WALK
(21 October 1927)

See the mountains! Like an artist's pallet
A radiant, effervescent mix of colours
As if a thousand painters had
Wiped their brushes on the landscape …

Gold and brown and red and ochre
Dotted on a canvass blue base
Like a woman's lustrous tresses.
Auburn hair that frames her face

Now harvest done, the terraced vines
Glow aflame in embers red
Ancient folk songs sung by vintners
Coursing through my blood and head.

Gentian blue, azure and clear
The firmament enfolds the day
You are beautiful and wondrous
And know nothing of death and decay

AFTERNOON IN MEERSBURG
(16 August 1928)

The silver threads are twisted and stretched
A thousand miles across the sea, etched
Into those summer midday hours,
Silence so shrill it almost hurts!

How the surface dances and sparkles in motion
As smooth as glass is now the ocean
No breath of wind fans the waves
Now wreathed in a distant bluish haze.

Leaning against the ancient monastery wall, I turn
And looking down deep in thought I yearn
Seeing a boundless sweet sorrow ...
I see happiness and a grave ... and await tomorrow".

A TRIP TO LAKE CONSTANCE
(16 August 1928)

Festive bells ring out to wake
The floating clouds in azure skies
Sailboats scudding on the lake
Gliding like white butterflies

Silence, mellow, deep and sweet
Comforting the waves where they meet
The radiant beauty in all its splendour
Drawing in the eye, beckoning and tender

Mountain and lake dressed for celebration
Pulsating summer heat, glowing with anticipation
Drink in the serenity, peace and joy unabated
Breathe in all this beauty till you are fully sated.

A PRAYER
(2 January 1928)

Oh God, let not your blessings be wasted
Here, bursting with life and the joy my heart has tasted,
Our urgent plea: "Save us from the violent mobs
Spoiling our daily lives with pain and fearful sobs."

"Let's hope for the best," I say a thousand times
And each time, the honesty of it chimes,
"Let's hope for the best" and from this ray of hope
Light comes to me when melancholy is my trope.

It is two worlds that must merge in all good grace,
But each of us inhabits our own singular space –
Moving closer at some instant of time but then
The loneliness descends again.

We cannot plumb the depths of another human being
Never understand all that we are seeing
This is my experience after a bitter, testing time
With that own beloved husband of mine!

BETROTHAL
(22 December 1928)

Come, give me your hand, my beloved,
Let us celebrate the feasts as they fall,
Every unused hour is time wasted,
For who knows when death may take us all.

Come, give me your hand, my beloved,
And let us share in sorrow and joy.
The wheel of life still turns
Come, smell the roses and enjoy.

Come, give me your hand, my beloved,
Our lights burn bright in our heart
We shall renew the oath we have taken
Let nothing ever prise us apart!

SEEDLINGS
Dedicated to Dr. Hugo Hahn[9]
(Cologne, 11 November 1929)

It was in those early years ...
When we were clay in potter's hand,
We were young and inexperienced,
And our souls uncultivated land.

Then you came and shaped the saplings
Each seedling growing into a tree
We drank in your spirit's gift,
And slowly became mature and free.

What ferments and drifts were in our souls,
So clouded, unclear, confused ...
You helped us through the torment of doubt
And on to new heights with brilliant light infused.

And what in long faded days
In soft earth was sown ...
Has blossomed and borne fruit,
And so in confidence we have grown

---

[9] Dr Hugo Hahn, born 1893 in Tiengen, 1915 pastoral rabbi to Offenburg, 1919 to Walldorf; liberal rabbi in Essen 1921–1939, then emigrated to New York; founded the German-Jewish community "Habonim" there in 1939 on the first anniversary of the night of pogroms; died 1965.

AFTER THE STORM
(1928)

Now the storm has run its course,
And puffs of cloud float by in liquid gold
The dark forests now are bathed in light
As if the savage storm had never been,
Had never shaken them, whipped them to the core,
Now they stand ... grave,motionless and serene.

The old brown farmhouse,
From whose eaves the rain dripped
Just now, it glows in the evening light
Bathing the windows in purple shadows.
The meadows are bursting with lush green life
Far away, two white clouds are drifting
Like pillows over the mountains, soft and warm
Now the vibrant, colourful rainbow arches
Its embrace framing the scene in a beautiful form!

FRAGMENT: ON THE OLD FAMILIAR PATHS
(undated)

On the old familiar paths
This morning I have seen
A thousand eyes ask anxiously
A thousand rain-spattered eyes complain:
It's so cold here!
Dear sun, when will you come again?

On the telegraph wires
Bright silver chains of droplets hang,
And a sudden whiff of roses from the west
Reminds us of the last rays
Of a day-weary sun.

Oh, I love these hours,
When, escaping from outdoors
We go inside and find ourselves
Lost in thought and talking quietly,
As the turmoil within us is calmed
And we bathe in the comforting warmth of our home,
Steeped in the heavenly peace that we love.

Yet the soul's quiet joy,
That we feel,
Is all too surely a harbinger
Of the death of the sweet summer.

FELDBERG
(November 1930)

My God! I am shaken to the core
By majestic heights the dark night renders
And my soul trembles in awe
At the sight of these heavenly splendours

When early in the twilight
The sun rises as the night withers
Then I awake, alone yet bright
And in that moment my soul quivers,

On the highest peak I stand
Filled with the beauty of the land,
Yet even in joy, just nearby
The loneliness of the universe greets me with a sigh.

FATE
(November 1930)

My heart is so sad,
What shall I do?
Life has lost its spark,
I can find no meaning in the dark

A sad little flower, hanging its head,
Who will revive it in its bed?
My heart is pierced to the core,
It beats wearily, hope is no more.

I have no tears,
My eyes are empty, wide with fears,
It is hard for me not to despise
The fate that evolves before my eyes.
Before, all around was bright,
Sparkling, glowing, dancing light,
But now is gone all that beauty
Just one thing remains: our duty!

NEW YEAR'S EVE 1930/31

The stars are so high
In this bright winter sky
So lonely, cold, no warmth they render
As they twinkle above in pitiless splendour.

Now by the window I stand
Looking at the firmament, brilliant and grand,
I'm shaken with fears and woe
How to carry on? This I don't know.

How come this year has so started?
All joy and warmth from the sun have departed
All beauty is gone and I am bereft
For Evil is all that is left.

You stars, so high in the air,
Tell me, is the new year set fair?
Will I praise it, or will it be a curse?
Will it be better or will it be worse?

Oh, stars above who are so timeless
I can forgive your deathly silence
If we knew what was to come tomorrow
There would surely be far greater sorrow!

FREIBURG
(18 August 1931)

Pain makes us cower and feel small ...
Yet there survives beneath it all
A little soul that wants to fly
To learn, to see beauty to gladden the eye
And to pass through life full of admiration –
Not with this feeling of desperation.

Now clouds are softly floating down
Obscuring the beauty all around
Leaving me no rest or peace,
Or endowing me with a joyful release
The blue sky has vanished in gloom
I see only dark clouds and with them, doom.
No shaft of blue, no comforting word of mirth,
As darkness descends upon the earth.

Ultimately we are all of us alone
Yet even when all hope has flown
Beneath the pain, as time goes by
There's a little soul that wants to fly!

Early poems 1919–1933

TO FATHER ON HIS 71ST BIRTHDAY
(22 July 1931)

Dearest Daddy, this is your very special day
But hardly a joyful one unbounded
Hard times have left us all confounded
All our happiness has been snatched away.

And yet, despite the hardships, cares and woe
I want to give thanks to our good Lord today.
Who gave enough bread for what is to come our way
And is a rock that never wavers or brings us low.

Here, in good health, vibrant, in the family fold
Sits the father of children and oh! what a crowd,
While you reside at our table, warm and proud
The harshest of winters will never be cold.

For your love is the very bond
That binds us together for ever and well beyond!
So give me your hand, my Daddy dear,
Stay with us, God willing, and we'll never know fear.

I WANDER THROUGH FLOWERING MEADOWS
(Ühlingen in the Black Forest, 17 May 1930)

I wander through flowering meadows
Till I reach the edge of the forest.
There, I greet the sun kissed day
The first good one I've had this May.

I can still see droplets of rain gleaming
On the blossoms and grasses
As if the shining fields anew
Are still bathed in morning dew.

Once more, my heart beats faster,
For after the dull grey of the rain
The bright sky above displays its hue
Radiant in its glorious robe of blue!

NOW I HAVE ALREADY GLIMPSED THE SPRING
(Ühlingen, 17 May 1930)

I have already glimpsed the spring,
And it gladdens my heart to see
I can again attend the birth
Of new life emerging.

How good feels the early summer light
Cast on meadows clothed in gold
I drink in the scenic picture, and yet …
I cannot enjoy it to the fullest

Lurking behind lush greenery
In the play of light and shade,
I see dark shadows looming
Over sunlit mountain pastures

But the blossom trees direct
Their luscious fragrance fast into the light
Spring fever grips me and I am overcome
And thankful for these blessings!

My heart is filled with joyful gratitude
These halcyon days do resonate
They help me to restore
The balance of the scales.

No longer sick, though the suffering
Has not completely faded
But the soul is soothed

By the blessed bridge that formed
Between my pain and my pleasure.

Oh, the rigid routine of the working day
Or learning something new
For me, I am happiest here in the grass
In the forest, with the heavens shining down on me!

BREATHING SPACE
(Ühlingen, 18 May 1930)

The grey days, so lovely and so vibrant,
When the forest stands quite silent,
When lustreless and uncomplaining
The day is slowly waning.

In twilight, the lush green landscape rests in slumber
The gentle breeze does not disturb or encumber
I hold still, waiting to hear the cry
Of a wild bird calling nearby
Unsettled by the wind's lament
Otherwise … silence, heaven sent!

The earth observes the Sabbath quest
And keeps this as a day of rest
Sent to restore its joie de vivre
Here's new vigour and the promise of spring fever!

EASTER SUNDAY
(Gengenbach, 19 April 1930)

Church bells ring out their sad song
The rain persists as the day is long
Banks of mist, wisps of cloud
Hang over mountain and valley like a shroud.

Sadly stand the blossom trees
Bright blooms shivering in the breeze
No sunlit spring dreams now to enjoy
They vanished – as did all their joy!

In the lime tree a blackbird sings
Of the hope that Easter brings
He perches in his leafy pulpit high
Celebrating Easter Day with his sweet cry

EASTER MONDAY
(Gengenbach, 20 April 1930)

What has happened in this night?
The earth awoke rejuvenated and bright,
On mountain and valley the sun is at its height
The radiant splendour of spring so fair
Beckons me out to share the air!

Yesterday was dull and dismal,
I recall it being quite abysmal
Yet the blackbird's song of joy and gladness
Makes my heart sing and banishes sadness.

The blue skies now are clear and bright
Lady sun radiates her golden light
Over lush green meadows that delight.

The blossom trees bask in the change
The world so golden now, so strange
As if long gone is yesterday
A day so full of damp and grey

Once again, the bells are ringing
A different song today they're singing
It penetrates my soul with its perfection
Recalling the joy of resurrection!

Now I know that Easter has arrived
With the warmth which is from the sun derived
Now kissed awake is all the earth
Lustrous, clad in spring's robe of rebirth.

A RETURN TO HEALTH
(Gengenbach, 20 April 1930)

I lie in the flowering garden,
Where all is new and beautiful
And my senses are alert, expectant,
As if something is about to occur.

I close my eyes and take in
The fragrant balm of the blossoms.
I know not what they're good for …
Other than to inspire sweet thoughts of mine!

I hear the melodious sounds
Of the feathered choir's chorus –
And from deep within my being
There bursts forth exultant joy!

A BOND FOR PEACE
(December 1931)

Women! Join hands with your sisters
To form a bond across the globe
A sisterhood to put an end to war
And make the great covenant of peace!

Let the spirit of love rule,
Instead of discord, conflict and strife,
Come, deny Mars, god of war, his spoils
Now and for all eternity.

Did you raise your children
To go to war and fight?
Let them live and flourish in peace,
And keep them from a darker fate.

Tie the ribbons and close the chain
That links us far across sea and land,
Only blessed peace can save us now
The bond that should unite us all.

THE FINAL MILE …
(18 November1932, on the death of Father)

It was on a bright November day,
That he quietly left us and passed away.
He lay in peace upon his bed …
But left us in such fear and dread.

Later in the dark evening hour
Male friends came sombre and dour
They struck the most painful blow that could be
As I watched them take my father from me

How could they remove him while I am forsaken
In silence in the home from which he was taken
To live seventy years here was his fate
Now, it is only a black hearse that awaits.

The long procession of mourners so solemn
Came to escort him in a long column
Soon the velvety darkening mantle of night
Enveloped those weeping in the twilight

The rhythm of horses hooves, the clatter of feet,
Broke the silence that day in the street
Only the luminous moonshine gave some relief
To comfort us in our hour of grief

To stop a sob escaping as I stand
I'll clamp my mouth shut with my hand
God grant him rest – and be content –
So ends his earthly life of torment.

Poems
1933–1940

A common woe

BROTHER!
(July 1933)

And for this did you go through the war,
That they mock your nose and close their door
Brother, I mean you

You offered your life in the storm like the rest
And you were among the strongest and best
That saved Germany from foreign invasion,
Then, not "foreign" you, but your home nation
Brother, I mean you

Now you are off to another land
Your suitcase packed, held in your weary hand
Your soul is heavy, you have lost your home
Who would do that for a future unknown?
Brother, I mean you

Sad eyes your deep sorrow do betray
Seeing how it was then and how it is today
Brother, I mean you!

ZION
(10.9.1933)

Homeless we have become,
Wandering over land and sea
Deep in the south, high in the north,
No one, not one nation willing to take us in.

Did not God give our ancient forefathers
A land flowing with milk and honey?
Blue and white is its flag
And Eretz Israel is its name.

Land of life, land of joy,
The light of our future,
To you we look in sorrow:
Do not send us away. Take us in.

After all the gloom there shines a bright star
A glimmer of hope for all those of us in need
Zion – home, to love you
Is our most sacred commandment!

WHO IS A HERO?
(11.9.1933)

Who is a hero? Is it he who overcomes his own nature?
Surely the words we hear these days
Are sounding a warning bell?
What good is endless lamentation now?
It is our duty to courageously bear
What fate imposes on us
We young people want to be brave
But proclaiming it alone will not do
We must grit our teeth
Work our fingers to the bone
We'll lift and carry with arms and hands
And lay the foundations piece by piece
To build our future in this promised land
And trust in God.
Amen to that! And every child
Shall be proud that we are Jews.

JEWISH WOMAN IN A JEWISH HOME
(September 1933)

The husband spends his time with the Kehilla[10]
Seeking religious knowledge and spiritual salvation
While at home in blessed silence and without restraint
The wife is busy doing the chores with ne'er a word of complaint

She is the pillar of the home and her role
Is to be its spirit, its heart and soul
The mother, come sun, wind or rain
Is always there for adult and child in both joy and pain.

She teaches us to keep the mitzvot[11],
Out of pious duty – forced to, we're not
She must make the festivals a time so beautiful
Especially the sabbath, as a Jewish wife most dutiful

She does her duty, despite burdens and woes
Devoted to duty, always working as she goes
And every new morning in every case
She shows us a happy, smiling face.

She is the priestess at the hearth,
Radiating goodness and peace, showing us the right path
Let us become Jewish mothers, wherever we roam,
And Jewish women in a Jewish home!

---

[10] Hebrew "assembly": Name of the Jewish community
[11] Hebrew commandments

TO GERMANY
(6 August 1933)

In pain and in fear
I ask why I was ever born here
A thousand tears run hot down my face
For all that I will have lost in this place.

I love you, land, forest and lake
Your majestic mountains must I now forsake?
My heavy heart is breaking with sorrow
Fearful for what awaits me tomorrow

So you will no longer be my home?
The country that I love is no more my own?
My injured soul will yearn for you
When I have to leave and say adieu

Your blood and mine may not be the same
The bloodline of this land I cannot claim
I know there's much that us divides
But stronger still is the bond that unites

This soil that is my lifelong home,
The much-loved earth I love to roam
How is it that I can suddenly be
A stranger in my own country?

I love you! Tormented to understand
That my people are no longer welcome in this land
Must be a Jew …must be from a different clan
And thereby you separate man from man.

THE CONSOLATION OF SPRING
(1934)

On the table laid with white linen
Stands the flat, green dish
Rim-full of spring blossoms
And deep inside my soul
I long for the peace of spring
After this long winter chill.

How they bloom! Fragrance fills the air
Oh! No one can take this away from us,
We can still admire the blossoms
And hear as from a clear blue sky
A blackbird sings out to welcome spring

May his song reach my heart,
Let me only see the golden sun
Hang low over the mountains
Whose dark and silent majesty
Is witness to our hearts' woe
Like a faithful watchman:
God made them for us too

In the silence, I bend my back
And my heavy burden is made lighter.

PEACE
(1934)

We who have no peace and no foundations
Are as a leaf carried on the wind among the nations,
We who are hated and shunned by all,
Yearn only for peace. That is our call
They even deny us this despite our cries
We are now just strangers to mock and despise

IN MEMORIAM THEODOR HERZL[12] AND CHAYYIM NAHMAN BIALIK[13]
(undated, ca. 1934)

We had men, courageous and strong
With lofty aims who accomplished great things
While one of them achieved by his deeds
The other proclaimed with poetry and writings

The leader Herzl, transformed into a figure of light
Appealed to the people with the purity of his soul
He united the defeated people as one
And showed the way, saying: "Here, Jew, choose!"

"Do you want to continue living in *galuth*, exiled[14]
As the pariah of nations, in perpetual suffering?
Or prefer to rejoice in the bright dawn of a rising sun?
And tread the path of hope? "

Then the disconsolate people cheered him loudly
And with renewed hope they shouted
"Show us the way, be our guide,
Fulfil your purpose and lead us to redemption!"

He took a path so thorny and barbed
And like Moses before him, took the people with him,

---

[12] Theodor Herzl (1860–1904), father of Zionism
[13] Chaim Nachman Bialik (1873–1934), popular Hebrew poet
[14] Hebrew: "Banishment"; designation of the exile and the Diaspora of the Jews in the countries outside Israel

As they murmured and quarreled and fought now and
    then.
He led the people, but in the end, like Moses, he too
Was deprived of his Canaan, the promised land.

He died too soon. A oak cut down by lightning.
But his spirit remains and he leaves us his legacy
Through him alone in all the world
In spite of the suffering and hardship: we have a home.

The other, Bialik the poet, was a herald, a prophet,
Guardian of the ancient wisdom that is our heritage.
No longer with us, his warnings and words now silent
Who shall protect the people's souls from ruin?

He lived life as a poet and a prophet,
Master of speech and writing in the holy language.
He took on the mantle of spiritual leadership
And made it his own life's work.

He too is dead. His mouth is now forever silent.
These two who gave us so much wisdom and beauty.
We think of them both in this grave hour:
Be they, their lives and deeds our role models.

TO FRITZ (BEFORE MAKING ALIYA[15])
(Autumn 1934)

In the little book of Jewish songs
That shows where your heart belongs
And by your loving aunt was found
Another song will now resound.

Let me tell you without further ado
Now is the time to say adieu
Let us not not complain or fear
A new life now begins right here.

You come here with love in your heart
To our sacred land, to make a fresh start
Let your joy banish all darkness from this land
And let it vanish to nothing in your hand.

Your life will be tough
The work will be hard and rough
But keep your faith good and true
And victory will surely see you through.

The sun may beat down till you blister and burn
Callused and cracked your poor hands will turn
Nothing will break your spirit now free:
Your blood, sweat and tears are all for our country.
But never forget or lose your way
At work, at study or at play

---
[15] Hebrew term for immigration to Palestine and Israel

You cannot know how sharp the pain
As you depart and I remain

You leave behind a most loving heart
As the land of your birth you now depart
A heart that suffers such sorrow and pain,
And is filled with yearning to be happy again.

A heart that is bound forever to you
In separation, struggle and sorrow too
A heart that wants to share the delight
In the joy of your life despite its plight.

When all the struggles are overcome
The hardships defied for a good outcome
With success hard won over every other
Please don't forget your loving mother.

RESIGNATION
(8 April 1935)

For hours I wrote,
Wrote till my heart was warm …
What is left of all this?
Impoverished I have become.

Rich, colourful pictures that
Float past my mind's eye
Trying to show me my youth
That may now be over …

May be? No! Is over! I am resigned
And I am not afraid
I have borne much,
My duty is to wear it lightly

I have grown tough and hard
I have been weaned off song,
Blossoms and leaves have withered
In vain, all my longing.

DISAPPOINTMENT
(8 April 1935)

How silent the hours creep,
The days so long and so bleak,
Seven days making up the week,
My sadness I can hardly speak

As for my daily life so stressed
Some meaning to it is addressed
When I feel low and distressed
Comes the Sabbath when I feel blessed.

The Sabbath marks the long week's end
The bleak days into one another blend,
To feel you near I pretend
To sense the kisses that you send.

I shall wait the many weeks through
Hoping and yearning soon to see you
I do not bake or cook as I used to
Gladly I did these things to honour you.

When that sabbath comes, dark thoughts I banish
And we're really together, yet I feel the anguish
You are remote and distant, and there I languish
You're present in body, but in thoughts you vanish.

To lean my body against yours I ache,
To feel the comfort from you that I take
Only tears I have left, weeping for your sake
Leaving me with painful heartbreak.

This plague of a life has conspired
To make you weary, worn out and tired,
So that your eyes no longer see or admire
My joy in you and my desire.

The days of the weeks are long, I profess
Filled as they are with loneliness
Sunday's made longer by my distress
And the disappointment, sorrow and stress.

COME, DEAREST, LET US RETURN SOON
(1935, tenth wedding anniversary)

Come, dearest, let us return soon
To the fresh spring when we were young married.
Even if life has shattered many a dream,
And has not lived up to our high ideals,
...
Apart from learning about the world around us
We also got to know ourselves
...
Well, darling, a union that lasts 10 years
Shall not be parted when we reach 20!

JEWISH WOMAN IN A WORLD-FAMOUS SPA
(Baden-Baden, August 1936)

I know you wherever we meet –
The tired old grief-stricken woman I greet,
I know you wherever we meet
By your sorrowful eyes that signal defeat.

I know you when I even hear your tone
As you speak the language of the land as your own,
For your voice is heavy with scars and enshrines
The fate of the Jews and you, the victim of crimes.

HAPPY CERTAINTY
(12 June 1937)

I exult and carry my head high,
And proclaim it loud and clear –
Our Lord God is just.

How they spit and rage
But one day they will give up
And then they will suffer.

Those who hate instead of love humanity
Who with knowledge practise only evil
Their good times will die overnight

In humility I will wait,
Till God's sun will once again
Shine upon my garden

CHORUS
(undated)

Brother, sister, reach out your hand!
Bound by one bond, an unbroken band
Fate's hard fist has rained down hard and long
But still we stand here, proud and strong
We are chips off our forefathers' sturdy block
Pressure or force will never destroy our stock.
As cheerfully we go on our way
Defying death and destruction come what may
We'll just keep on making bread!

We, who are the younger generation
Will no longer be blind to our situation
We are the heirs, our people the legatee
Of our fathers' long and tortuous history
May their suffering and ours not make us numb
But prepare us for what is yet to come.
Old blood, new strength contains
Lifeblood coursing through our veins
We are your seed: we are the Jews
Strong for action, not a moment to lose.

TZEDAKAH[16]

Charity is a duty for us Jews
Give what you can and not what you choose
For it is God who has commanded us

To give to the poor but without any fuss
To make our lives count is our creed
For the need of the poor is also our need

Let us give with a glad heart and mind
Let us not leave the poor behind
Though we cannot change with our donation
The fate of those who come to us in supplication. –

Therefore let them weep no more in desperation
'All for one and one for all' is an end to privation
This is Jewish help in action and our salvation.

---

[16] Literally "justice": used as a term for charity

KEHILLA[17]

A dying father spoke thus to his sons most dear:
'Go bind me some sticks and bind them tight
Stay as close as this no matter how others may jeer
Never be defeated, stay united, stand and fight'

Kehilla! Community! That's the idea
We need it twice as much in these times of fear
And if one of us perchance may stumble or fall
The community comforts, supports and gives joy to all

We must stay closer now, without a doubt
Family members, young and old, must now reach out
In trust and confidence for peace of mind
Necessity and need are the chains that bind

We need to close our circles tight
Kehilla – community – can keep us warm at night
When our brothers and sisters unbreakable bonds create
Then will it be easier to bear our fate.

---

[17] Hebrew "assembly": Name of the Jewish community

ALIENATION
(Breitnau, 6 June 1937)

How strange have I become
How fixed and so unlike myself
That now I must be without words
Without words – as if somehow taken from myself.

Me, who loved the winter's muted sounds,
The bird's rejoicing,
The flowers of the meadow in full bloom
That could seduce me to write poetry.

Me, in the dark pine forest's hills,
In the Black Forest deep and dense ...
There, lifting my spirits
From the gloomy sphere of earth.

Me, who loved the meadows
The bright meadow blossom,
The clouds that drifted in the sky,
Making my soul glow with joy

I feel as if a veil now hangs
Like a curtain over the earth,
As if it were now another thing
That no longer belonged to me

Still I see all that lives there,
Trees, plants, creatures and meadows.
I can still feel the vibrant summer
And recall the taste of its sweetness ...

Yet when I try reaching out to touch it,
All the glory that I owned as mine
A strange quiets creeps around me,
And the land is shrouded in silence.

I NO LONGER HAVE A FATHER OR MOTHER
(undated)

I no longer have a father or mother,
I have no one on earth, there is no other
With whom I could feel really safe
And not be just a father and motherless waif.

Oh, a mother oneself one may be
I have my own children three,
And a husband – and yet I am so alone,
Like birds in the snow, chilled to the bone.

It's not so bad when the daily grind
Keeps me busy and resigned
Then I forget the emptiness of this place
Hours when domestic duties fill the space.

But when with a soft beat of wings
The night descends and brings
An end to the activities of the noisy day
All is silent, hushed and grey.

Then my love-hungry heart pounds
With such terror that its beat resounds
It aches in pain – and the shibboleth
It thinks to see is impending death.

Oh, a mother onself one may be
And have a husband and children three
But in the depths one may be as alone
As starving birds in winter when summer has flown.

LET YOURSELF GO …
(9 June 1937)

For once, without the weight of my burden
For once, I belong only to myself,
And all dissonant notes are silent.

The soft breeze whispering over the hills
Triggers a yearning in me …
And I can already hear the question.

Let yourself go, let yourself sink –
You will never drown
In the dark torment of the night,

Everything will be easier,
Never will I lie sleepless,
Or sink down into the black hole.

No one will fall into the void,
And my own weight will surely
Bring me back from the brink.

Sun, sky and the wind singing
Carry me on the wings of angels
On the path to strength and happiness!

FEAR OF PEOPLE
(10 June 1937)

It would be unbearable, I must bemoan
After these short days on my own
Were I no longer to be alone

Those lovely summer hours of old
Finding who I am, not what I'm told
Is worth more to me than gold

Shall I be lost in the endless void?
My peace of mind be so destroyed
I must be alone, all people to avoid.

The monotonos drone of human sighs
Talk of a thousand woes and troubled lives
Pours forth ... and something in me dies.

In the cacophany of noise, I do plead
For that soft silence of a summer's day I need
In lush green meadows, there I shall be freed.

To smell fragrant fields, I yearn and long
To hear the birds as they sing their sweet song
But people? Preserve me from the babbling throng!

SUMMER
(1937)

Only in summer comes that sensation
Of floating, carried off on a tide of elation
Every cloud is a revelation
And the green earth – a carpet in my imagination.

Weightless, when everything is light
In these hours of sheer delight
The soul floats weightless in the air,
And the heart is freed from all despair.

IN SIGHT OF HAPPINESS
(Ravenna, 11 June 1937)

As I walk one summer's day
I meet a young couple along the way
Their eyes shining, of all around, they're unaware
Those beautiful bodies and sun-warmed hair.

How they walk through the days
Drunk with love, at each other they gaze,
Such pleasure and joy in each caress
And life seems to be pure happiness.

There they are and I catch sight
As they wait in penumbrate twilight
In married bliss as day gives way
To the crowning glory of each day.

Oh, to always see their happiness
That all-embracing tenderness
For it is their mutual faith and trust
That satisfy my own needs as they must.

FEAR

Sister, you have gone away …
Gone, good friends who did not stay …
Now I am chilled to the very bone
Will I soon be all alone?

Every day, some links do crumble
Breaking ancient chains as they tumble
Will I see you again, dear sister blessed
Before I go to my eternal rest?

Wander, wander, we must wander
The curse of homelessness we ponder
Marriages are torn apart,
Destroyed in body, soul and heart.

Oh Lord, please leave me what is left
Take not my husband and children and leave me bereft
If we have to wander forever,
I pray you, let us do so together!

SPRING 1938 FOR CITY JEWS

How painful, all this blossom and beauty,
Springtime in our malignant world
Decked out in withered garlands, these urban Jews
With flowers that droop their wretched heads

They still live in a world of yesterday
Playing with the dog, going out for coffee,
And yet we are all brothers and sisters
That share a common woe.

It's all a masquerade and posturing
They put on an act and all is make-believe
What they were has vanished into the abyss
What they are, is not what they would wish to be.

They languish on benches in beautiful avenues
Not old and retired, but with time on their hands
You see them strolling in the spring-fresh streets,
But their eyes betray that they are lost and distant

How painful is all the blossom and beauty
Here is life but all around the world is dying
There are no more heads to wear a crown of flowers
And no one to comfort the fallen.

ROLL CALL[18]
(1938)

They stand in the night in rows in their thousands
Freezing, shivering and listening intently
Who will be among the lucky ones today?
Entire lives hanging on the words they hear.

They stand in the night in rows in their thousands
Our brothers dressed in their thin rags
Do you not hear their souls crying?
"Count them off, the Jewish rabble!"

One name rings out, then another
Friend, brother, whomever – off they go
Then hearts become heavy and leaden
And you must stand and listen and wait.

The night is fading, the mist rolling in.
The sun will soon be rising in the east
My heart grows sore and cold with dread
And I ask myself how long must I bear it.

Our brothers are lined up in rows in their thousands,
Hearts and hands clenched tight in fear
"When will my turn come?"
The great roll call is over for another day.

---

[18] Deportation of the male Offenburg Jews in November 1938 ("Kristallnacht") to Dachau

FOR FRAU DR. STEINHARD[19], MUNICH
(1939)

Little woman with warm heart
Agile in spirit and mind that's smart
Reaching out to a woman in need and pain
A sisterly hand of friendship, making her whole again.

More than just shelter for exiles she provides
Bed, room, cosy hearth and more besides
Loving words and a welcome that's warm
Is our sanctuary from the gathering storm.

---

[19] In a letter to Dr. Steinhard, Tengstr. 27, where Sylvia Cohn took refuge in Munich in 1939, when the communities close to the border with France were evacuated into the interior of the Reich when war broke out

SINCE YOU LEFT ME
(9 February 1940)[20]

Since you left me
Homeless I have wandered
From place to place, ever onward
No rest or respite, nor am I free

Since you left me,
Life is empty and I'm bereft
No help, no comfort, nothing left
Weighed down by sorrow, nor am I free

Since you left us
Parted by more than sea and land
While warring armies fight hand to hand
You there, me here, nor am I free

Since you left me
The world's in tumult where
War cries and cannon fill the air
My ship is rudderless, nor am I free

Is that why you left me,
I left you in spirit, die you grieve?
And is that why you had to leave?
Because my heart broke faith with you?

---

[20] Eduard Cohn emigrated to England in May 1939

And now because we're far apart
Ed, you cannot see the longing in my heart
So homesick for you that I think I'll die
If no one hears my anguished cry

And I am so forsaken
So eerily alone and shaken
Ed, I simply cannot see
Why this situation has to be

Evenings with the lamplight glowing
When I'm reading, writing, sewing
That's when I feel that you are nearest
And I'm not alone, my precious dearest

And the heart, so sweetly beguiled
When I write letters, it feels not exiled
Or sad deprived of all the joy and gladness
And that it must remain alone in sadness.

THE STORM IS RAGING, THE NEED IS GREAT
(16 February 1940)

The storm is raging, the need is great,
I am abandoned, poor, bleak and left to my fate
Will no one free me from this parlous state?

The wind is howling and dark is the sky
We are one body, my child and I
Child, cry help! Louder must we cry

The cries die away but undeterred
Persisting, hoping our cries may yet be heard
But stone has no ears and hears no word

Kneel with me, my child, and pray
Cry out to God for his help this day
Help, Lord, for we are lost in the fray.

Poems
1940–42

On 22 October 1940, Sylvia and two of her daughters, Myriam and Eva, were deported and taken to the French camp in Gurs, South of France together with the other Jewish people from Baden.

IN THE CAMP HOSPITAL

A heart that has beaten since birth
And carried the heaviest burden of duty
Cried out to be saved, loveless now
But no one, no one heard
And so her warm heart grew cold
And soon from her her lips
Came the sound of bitterness and anguish
Now the woman lies alone in the ward.

Visitors chat, they come and go
What does André know of your woes?
Bed twenty is silent, a tear wells up
But no one sees, not man, not child.
She looks at two pictures, eyes brimming with tears,
The man and the children, yet no one else

And yet, yet she is …so alone
The sun streams in through the windows
Visiting hours are over and people are leaving
Bed twenty can no longer bear to look
Quiet, her head in her hands
She turns to face the wall
Visiting hours are over!

ED, YOU CANNOT SEE IT
(13 November 1941)

Ed, you cannot see it
But my heart is consumed with homesickness.
Ed, I will surely perish
If no one hears my cry for help.

Ed, I'm so forsaken –
So utterly, eerily alone,
Ed, I can't believe
Why it had to be like this.

In the evening by lamplight
When I'm writing, sewing, reading
I'm not so much alone
As you are with me, my dearest ones.

And the heart, sweetly beguiled
Does not feel so alone when I am writing …
Not weighed down by the memory of past happiness
And the knowledge that it must remain alone.

Dearest, I have your photograph with me
And I look into your eyes
Until my eyes well up with tears
And I can no longer see to write.

But then, when in the endless night
A deep blackness oppresses me,
My heart awakes with grief
And my soul is ripped apart by sorrow.

I feel the dreadful pain,
I cannot pretend that it is not so:
I am trapped and quite alone
Alone, in my deep distress.

A FAREWELL TO MISS DALLHEIM
(3 December 1941)

You have yearned so long and been so glum
For what you thought might never come
Now at last your wish comes true
Ring out the old, ring in the new.

What we have suffered is inhumane
Torment, anguish, misery and pain.
And yet we bore it, both women and men
Now I am alone again.

But it is not sadness that I feel
Though the pain of parting is very real
Go, go, go, go, go, go, go, and please –
Save yourselves, go overseas.

And tell them all a thousand times
Tell of our suffering and their crimes
Hunger, cold, hardship, they take no heed
Torment us, plague us, watch us bleed.

Shout it out, friends, and shout it loud
Wake up the doves in every crowd!
That they may see this unhappy throng
And save us, but tell them not to wait too long.

Save us before it is too late
Help us, do not leave us to our fate
Do not wait, and now hear our lament
For murder is their true intent.

(SIXTY WOMEN ON SIXTY PALIASSES)
(undated)

Sixty women on sixty paliasses of hard straw
Wind howling round the barracks, cold and raw
And we cannot tell the day from night
Because both the doors are shut tight
This cursed damp around us wraps
Its icy fingers through a thousand cracks
Penetrating through blanket, coat and dress
Chilled to the bone to our distress
On sixty paliasses sixty women are trying
To stifle the muffled sounds of their crying
Shivering, cold and fearful, hoping for a better tomorrow
As they press their hands to their mouths in sorrow.

THE FIRST DAY OF THE FESTIVAL OF SHAVUOT[21]
(June 1941)

Carry my greetings, Oh wind,
To you, my husband, to you, my child!
The knowledge that at this precise same hour
All the consecrated will hear the familiar melodies
That bind us together across land and sea
Making my heavy burden seem lighter today
Though homesickness consumes me.
Onward, radiant azure skies …
Only the soft music of flowers tinkling in the breeze
Is our choir in services now
And the gentle sea that borders
Our homeland shines …
Rejoicing the eye and lifting us up.

Just a small table in the meadow
A beggar's table, yet on it, sweet treasure
Our Torah, our precious holy jewel
And in deepest tones of supplication
We poor souls are intoning an appeal and
Beseeching God with heavy hearts.

---

[21] Shavuot: Festival of Weeks. Middle of the three major festivals of the year, Succoth – Harvest Festival (in Christianity celebrated as Pentecost

Oh, the men and Oh, the women,
Their eyes are hot with tears
As they look up to God on high:
Emaciated, haggard, hungry and wretched
WIth a thousand woes and sorrows
Already etched on their faces.

Children, young, whose eyes set deep
Peer out from hollow cheeks
Sitting silent, pale and still
A festival! So? They should be praying
But a thousand woes and hardships ...
And they no longer trust in God.

Almighty Father, hear my cries
When, Oh when will You set us free?
When will You hear our fervent pleas?
A festival! The melodies, ancient and familiar
Rise up to heaven in supplication and yet
We cannot see God.

20 DECEMBER 1941, CHANUKAH –
THE CAMP INFIRMARY[22]
(Memories of the events of the past two years since Eduard's return from Dachau at Chanukah 1938)

Once, Oh God – you heard me
As I lay crushed and writhing in agony:
"Give me back my man! It cannot, it must not be
That malice, hatred and savage fury
Will break this small, poor ship of life in two.
Give me back my husband!" – Then you heard me
You gave me a golden day in the depths of winter

With a despondent heart I stood, drawing my children near
In despair, burying my head in their brown and blond hair
And our tears flowed, we could not hold them back,
"Our God in heaven, give us back our father!"
The day was grey and gloomy, the snow kept falling
And anguish was raging in our sore souls.

Suddenly I heard the cry: "Mummy, oh, Mummy –
Daddy's come home!" Is it possible …?
I jumped up, flew to the door and took him in my arms,
So thin, so degraded, so tormented and full of grief.
The man who never cries, cried now

---

[22] Chanukah "Inauguration": Festival of light in memory of the temple consecration (roughly at the same time as the Christian Christmas); Eduard had returned from Dachau on the Chanukah festival in 1938. Infirmary: Sickbay

My tears flowed too, from the bottom of my heart.
But what happiness I felt! My heart jumped for joy,
I thanked our God, who saved me from my sorrow
I have you again! Never mind the snow! Never mind this
  winter day..
Such a memorable winter day
You have come home to me! Now, come what may
And what I feel so keenly and the heartfelt thanks
I see reflected in my children's eyes, radiating like
  sunshine.

I prepared for the festival as if in a dream
The most delicious, the best was hardly good enough
To grace the table today, for today is a festival, a holy day
And I wanted to be happy, hoping that my troubles were
  over.

So deeply had I suffered for you, my beloved husband,
That I firmly believed nothing could separate us now.
Oh, God! It was only a trick of the light: false hope of my
  childlike heart
I little thought the wound would open once again
And inflict on me the deepest pain.

Then came the golden spring and the beautiful month of
  May
And my little ship of life broke in two once more
You left! I stood abandoned with my children
With strangers who hated me and no one near to me.
You left! I couldn't believe it: you left us all alone
Deaf to all my pleas, my cries and my appeals.

A storm arose in the sky, the savage war broke out
The bloody tumult of battle chases us from home and
  hearth

The mother ties scant possessions in a bundle
Takes her children by the hand
Weeping, she leaves behind all that she knew as home
This war has forced thousands to flee
To try and find food and shelter.

Filled with strong emotion, I think of the many noble
    women
Jewish women, brave sisters who eased my suffering
For it was not only bread and shelter they offered
They gave me their hearts
And so helped the poor to bear their pain.
The months flew by and then they sent us back
And we came home to find all in its place there
Nothing, not a single item, was missing and yet
It was so cold, so empty
Without the head of the house, the father
It no longer felt like home.
I rearranged the rooms, I moved things hither and thither
But nothing, nothing helped. The father was missing.

So I took my children and fetched a bouquet of flowers
Hoping in my heart it would bring sunshine into the
    house
The blossoms shone brightly – a feast for sore eyes,
But no peace came to the heart, no joy to the soul.

So day after day, night after night crept by,
My soul full of grief and trouble , my mind full of sorrow.
Separated from my children by the evil that is Hitler
I had no choice but to send them to a school far away
Leaving me to suffer from morning till night.
I felt so forsaken, so solitary and alone
I could not believe that this was meant to be.

The devil tightened the screws, pursuing us
The constraints we are subjected to have grown harsher
The longer the war dragged on, the worse the devil made it for us
He tortured us, he beat us, he taunted us, he made us suffer
He took from us what he wanted, our professions, assets and provisions,
Our jewels and our gold he plundered, leaving us in dire need.

And yet, in all the anguish of our souls, we held fast
The last thing we had: our sanctuary, our homes
While cannon thundered and roared and sirens screamed
We thought we were safe and trusted in God
The 'planes were dropping bombs, the war was raging,
And I felt safe: at home, protected in the haven of my home.
Then lightning struck …sudden and terrible
Even the last comfort of home was taken from us.
Once again, the devil hurled his poison arrows and once again
The Jews were the targets
Quietly I did my work until one day in late autumn
The devil's henchmen came to my room
"The creature comforts of your home are ended
Make haste, pack up your clothes, you have an hour
But leave all that is dear to you and valuable
I'll tell you straight: from now on
You'll learn the hard way. Mark my words."

Then in my shock, I felt no fear
"The children, my children, they are far from here
Do not separate me from my children, do not do this to me!"

And I begged on bended knee. "But you are a man and a
    human being"
But all my pleading did not move him: he had no pity for
    my plight
I was taken away an hour later.

This is how, with the bundle on my back, bag in my
    hand,
And a few morsels of bread, I left my home and country
My God, you saw what they did to us
You let it happen to husband, wife and child.

After many long hours of anguish and heartache
I found two of my little children on the train.
I thanked God, shaken. But my heart was sore indeed
Because I knew my third child was abandoned and alone
As a beggar with my bundle and two children out of three
I stood alone: no-one to protect us –
And all hope of happiness gone.

The dark train chugged through the pitch-black night
Taking a sad human cargo to the remote unknown
On and on we travelled by day and night
Through France's fair countryside
Until at last we reached our destination.

We were taken to a camp, deprived of all freedom,
Made sick and thin, our treatment became harsher
We tightened our belts and prayed to God …
Will this never end? And the misery just grew and grew
We were hoping for some of France's fabled humanity
But even here we encountered hatred and persecution.

O God! I saw my little children blanch,
Lose the bloom of their cheeks and to my infinite grief

I could not give them the bread which they craved
Gripped only by one thought of a hungry child in fear
I begged, I wrote, I pleaded, but much time passed
While the mother's heart stayed deep in distress
Until at last the children were released and taken
To safety in the nearby children's home
And now my heart's sorrow turned to the child left alone
Days and weeks pass and I am lost and forlorn
I cannot find peace: I have run out of hope.

The captivity lasts one and a quarter years
My hair has turned grey, my strength is gone
I am like a tree blown over by the wind in a storm
Oh Lord, help your child before it is too late
I am but a grain of sand in the icy cold sea
Hear, Oh God, hear me! Save me soon!
I am like a shooting star tumbling through space
Catch me in your arms, Oh God, and save me from the abyss.

How long shall I plead? Torn apart from husband and children
How long must I beg you to reunite us? Do You not see me?
How long must I atone for guilt unknown?
I prostrate myself at your feet, Lord God, grant me mercy
Today is the third anniversary of the most beautiful day of my life
When my husband came back to me and my torment seemed over
When will we, our children and I, have what we dare to dream …
To be happy in freedom?
When will the longed-for hour approach
The 20th December that binds what is divided?

When will I see you again, my beloved husband?
You and all my children, when will we be united?
Almighty God, tell me when?
When shall I ever again feel the greatest happiness on earth?
When will love return to my poor heart?

CAMP DE GURS, BASSES PYRENEES, BLOCK I/BARACK 8
(1940)

Hammering on the roof, I hear the rain
I lie in the straw, awake, and once again
I cannot sleep for all the pain.

Thunder rumbles and the storm rages
What have we done, Oh Rock of Ages
That our punishment is cruel and outrageous?

Tormented, in foul dirt we are tossed
We're lost …lost …so lost
We hunger and we pray to God aloft.

The rain is pouring through the night.
Oh Lord, how much longer can I fight?
Take it, take this life and release me from my plight.

MIRACLE IN RIVESALTES[23]
(11 March 1942)

Spring has come into my room,
My poor heart welcomed its golden bloom
It thawed and warmed my heart grown cold
So that it can trust again as of old
Now it does not feel alone or sad
Though it is – but now my heart feels glad.

In the camp, too, spring has awakened
Us, from whom all else was taken,
Of warm clothes, a bed, food, we are bereft
Only misery is what we have been left,
Where we step, just stones, more stones we see
How dismal and bleak can a land really be?

And yet! Spring has come to us too
Showing us the wonder of the sky of blue
We take heart as spring unfurls its warm fingers
And we hear the song of a blackbird as nearby it lingers
Oh blossoming tree in the warm sunlight
No, we have not been forgotten by God in His might.

---

[23] Many deportees were transferred from Gurs to Rivesaltes on the Mediterranean coast near Perpignan

BE STRONG, MY HEART
(11 March 1942)

Be strong, my heart and have patience
Even if your hunger remains unsatisfied
We are still only half way up the ladder
However gruelling, we must keep on climbing
And nothing, nothing is yet fulfilled

Be strong my heart and have patience
Only the driving force be the light of hope ...
You still must wait a long, long time
And bear all the many hard hardships
That fate inflicts, yet do not despair for me.

Be strong, my heart, and have patience
You must keep on and reach your goal
A rosy glow in the firmament
Gives a sign that all this suffering
Will come to an end.

In March 1942, Sylvia Cohn compiled a book of poems for her children Esther, Myriam and Eva. She called it "Of Yesterday and Today": "You know that I had to leave everything behind. (…) What I give you in this booklet, I wrote from memory, and it also brought to life many of the songs Mummy would sing to you!"

Eva Mendelsson: "The last song my mother sang with me was: "No fire, no coal can burn so hot, as secret love, of which no one knows". She taught me that, I remember us walking around the camp in Rivesaltes holding her hand. It is my last and most treasured real memory of my mother. Of course, she also left us her poems. When I read them, it's like having a conversation with her."

TO MY CHILDREN

(…)
Know that your mother loves you
And sends you her blessing,
And as you turn the pages
They will stir thoughts of "homeland"

Don't forget it:
Forget not the country of your birth
Let your mother tell you,
There was joy and light
In the life we once lived there.

Poems 1940–42

Of Yesterday and Today. A small anthology of poems for my beloved children from their mother. Rivesaltes Camp, 15 March 1942

Selected letters

Letter to elder sister, Hilde, in Palestine
(Saturday evening, 1 October 1938, Offenburg)

Hilde, my sister,

Ed went out to the Cafe Weil[24] and I'm sitting here at the table alone (the children are already asleep) with the sole aim for this evening of communicating with you, my dearest one.

The week ends today – a week that I, that all of us (= the family of Man) – will never forget. We were a mere hair's breadth from war, from the most horrible disaster that could ever happen...and we are here, so near to the border. Hilde, it was terrible. A thousand thanks to heaven that we can say: 'it WAS terrible'. The awful stress of the past weeks, then this dramatic week at the end of which I am writing to you and finally the eleventh hour meeting of the four leaders (*of Germany, France, Britain and Italy*) in Munich and finally yesterday, Friday, the relief of hearing that there has been a last minute agreement and there will be no war! Hilde, if thoughts could fly, then across the sea you would have heard the sigh of relief of our poor tormented souls here in Europe.

We are still trembling in our boots and our suitcases remain packed and ready, and we have not even put away

---

[24] Offenburg, Blumenstrasse 3; destroyed during the November Kristallnacht pogrom 1938, dissolved 1939

our clothes yet (only the most essential items anyway) and our hearts, our poor hearts knowing that for us, nothing has changed, and yet, our poor hearts dare to rejoice and breathe a deeply humble: 'Thank God!'

And so, out of this depressing scenario, the heart of your tired, ageing sister has succeeded in fluttering like a bird, silently and yet beating slowly as if it wished to fall asleep. I wish for nothing in the world as much as that – inner and outer – peace, for which my tormented soul yearns.

Offenburg, 28 December 1938

My Dearest Hilde,
I hope you have now received my card of 21 December, in which I told you in brief the good news of Ed's return home *(Eduard Cohn had been imprisoned during Kristallnacht, the night of the pogrom, on 9–10 November 1938 and deported to Dachau together with the other male Jews of Offenburg; the men were released after four to six weeks on the condition that they kept quiet about their experiences and prepared to emigrate immediately)*. The post has been very unreliable these past six weeks, so I was happy to receive 3 cards from you the same day! You should have received this letter earlier too. But I am rather confused about the dates and details, because since Ed's return, the joy and happiness of our "reunion" has put me in such a daze that I just couldn't get down to writing a proper letter, – and after the first days (which were certainly the happiest days of my life so far!!!), the work I had to carry out dealing with family business kept me really busy, as all of us are now here, including Myriam, who will probably leave for England on January 5 or 6. (...) Today we had the 4th funeral here in 6 weeks. It was also a transformative moment: it was the first time

we saw most of our kehilla (*community*) again – in the cemetery. Everything was wrapped in the shroud of winter, silent, white snow …

Eduard and Sylvia Cohn to Hilde, Offenburg, 22 May 1939
(Eduard Cohn was already assigned to a transport to England on 30/31 May 1939 and his departure was imminent)

Dear Hilde,
I thought it was wonderful that you took a train to go and see B.C. in the hope that he could do something for me. Many thanks for your efforts. I will be leaving for the camp in England in the next few days. The permit has arrived and although the exact date of departure has not yet been fixed, I suspect that the transport will leave shortly after Whitsun. We have to go to the Meinekerstrasse Office for the certificates, but the current situation is most unclear. Not a single certificate (*this is a document confirming an applicant's place number on the waiting list for emigration to a particular country*) scheduled for April has come to Germany, with most of them still in Eretz *(Palestine at the time, now Israel)* and a few for the chaluzim[25] on hachsharah[26] (*agricultural training programs – often in Denmark*) preparing to emigrate to Palestine. There is talk of around 75,000 certificates being issued in the next 5 years, and I should receive mine, according to assurances given by the Meinekestrasse Office. I will not stop reminding the Palestinian

---
[25] "Equipped"; member of the "Hechalutz": non-political world organisation for the preparation and vocational training of young Jewish people for a working life in Israels

[26] "Training"; term for agricultural or craft training of future Palestine pioneers

Authority of this assurance, because I want to be reunited with my family as soon as possible. As far as the camp is concerned, the Palestine Office has given an undertaking to the Authority to guarantee that I will be able to leave within 9 months at the latest. But it need not necessarily be 9 months. In the camp, languages are learned, and there is also the possibility of training for a profession. What I will actually learn is not clear to me. Now I have told you everything about me, but the most important thing is the fate of Sylvia and the children. At the moment all three are in Freiburg, that means until tomorrow. The children will arrive tomorrow and stay with their mum until 5th June. At the moment, it may be possible to place Esther and perhaps Mirzel in Denmark for 2 years. This is a unique opportunity and is only available to us because of a kindergarten teacher who is close to the youth welfare service, i.e. the Meinekestrasse authority. If it works out, both of them will then go to Denmark and will later come directly to Eretz. This being the case, if the waiting time is too long, I would then try to get my wife and Eva to England. The worst aspect of all this is the uncertainty.

We hear a great deal of news about Eretz on the radio these days. Oh, I can well understand the rejection of the White Paper and I also assume that this White Paper (*this probably refers to the MacDonald white Paper issued on 17th May 1939 which severely restricted Jewish immigration to Palestine as mentioned above to 75,000 over the next five years with further immigration dependent on Arab consent*) will suffer the same fate as the previous unfavourable report which I have lately been eagerly studying. In the case of the latter wretched report (*a report on Immigration, Land Settlement and Development, commonly referred to as the Hope Simpson Enquiry or the Hope Simpson Report, was a British Commission managed by Sir John Hope Simpson, established during August 1929 to address Immigration, Land Settlement and De-*

velopment issues in British Mandate Palestine as recommended by the Shaw Commission after the widespread 1929 Palestine riots), we said at the time that never in history has a state been created against the will of its citizens. At that time, the scope of the Jewish state was too small for us Jews, and today? If Arabs and Jews reject the Palestinian State as projected by the British, then this plan will never become reality. So what will happen? I believe that no nation has ever been gifted anything and I believe that the future of our Jewish State does not depend on commissions, nor on white papers or on reports; the final shape will depend on ourselves and on world events, which mankind is moving towards in giant strides. Your courageous children, dear Hilde, show the way. Conferences come and go, and the land taken is so well defended that it will never again be given up. All this is down to energetic people and here I congratulate Ernst and Fritz on their recent aliyah (*moving to Israel*) and wish them every success in their work to build up the country!

I will finish now, because my Sylvia, who is putting the finishing touches to my packing, which needs to be completed for customs on Friday, is getting impatient. With every good wish to you, Ernst and Fritz,
Yours, Ed

Good sis! I am really and honestly dead tired. But the letter must go, so that you don't have to wait any longer. Thank you very much, Hildele, for going to Tel Aviv! Ed is going to the camp after all! I am so sick and tired and people are telling me to 'be happy' when all the while I have to stay here all alone and abandoned. I am so afraid for our Irma, who is very ill with heart problems. I just wish she would be well again.

Postcard, Offenburg 16 July,1939

(...) Things are looking bleaker than ever for us at the moment. Illegal immigration, on which 100 curses, is still supported by certain ..., which is completely incomprehensible to me. The associations that support these activities should be banned. As always, decent folk are the ones to suffer most grievously (...) Hilde, it's nobody's fault how the strings of his soul are tuned, that's the instrument maker's responsibility. I wish I had an easier life myself, and didn't always have to go around with a lump in my throat and a stone in my heart!

Offenburg, 26.7.1939

Dearest Hildelein, I am using the quiet of the evening to write to you. The children are all home for the holidays. At first, after being solitary for so long, I really had to get used to all the work again. Well, I soon got used to that and am very happy to have them here. At least now I know once again why I get up in the morning and it does my heart good to have laughter, shouting and – life around me again. It will probably be the last time for a long time that we can be together like this, in our home and living "independently". I would like to have the gift that I have always lacked, to consciously enjoy the good times of life without the eternal foreboding of what will be in my heart, that Cassandra sense of impending doom, so that in future, I can use the memory of the good times as a reservoir of strength to draw on when necessary.

The children have grown up and thank God, they look good. They do so love being at home again, especially Esther, who has had enough of being away.

Unfortunately, in the meantime there has not been any progress on the Danish front. All we hear is that it hasn't been decided yet, that we have to be patient and wait, wait, wait. I don't have much hope for it any more. (…)

Ed has a great deal of work, a lot of language teaching and again, in his meagre spare time, he leads a Zionist group in the camp. I think he looks after the chalutzim (those moving to Israel to help establish modern agricultural settlements) and again and again he sings of all the comradeship. This, he says, is a wonderful chapter there. The other aspect that commands great respect and admiration is the English people's willingness to help, to make sacrifices and the human kindness shown to these refugees by the English. Ordinary Christian workers have 2 or 3 shillings deducted from their meagre weekly wages for the refugees, and children bring single pennies, as many as they can, to their teacher at school every week for the same purpose.

Teachers come from many kilometres away without any remuneration to teach the men English and languages. (…) Here, our community is rapidly melding together, although it is hardly a community these days. The next to leave will be Hans and his family and Ludwig and his family. Both of them will pack up next week and then move with all their belongings to my place until they leave. These days you have to be helpful in whatever way you can. Where are these people supposed to stay until they leave? Hotels have long been out of the question. And they cannot stay in any public parks either, first of all because it is too cold there at night and second, that is also no longer possible. Keep your fingers crossed, and luckily, I can stay here until I emigrate.

You live in Haifa now and I hope you've settled in well and found a nice place to stay. I have always liked Haifa. If only it were quieter there: the noise is horrible! (...) The possibility of America is once again on the agenda and I find myself in a state, as I often did as a child in a dream, in which I free float in space, gripped by terror, no ground under my feet, no hold in the air, and not even a destination in sight. Tell me yourself, Hilde, without criticising my "minor key soul", how would you feel in my place? The Lord God should help us. Let there be peace on this tormented planet, and may He grant each of His children a place to breathe. And now I must finish. Give my love to your sons, with love and kisses. Yours, Sylvia.

Offenburg, 16 August 1939

Dear, dearest Hilde, in spite of my bone tiredness and my unspeakably aching feet (I was with Estherle in Gengenbach and from there we walked deep into the wonderful forest, because Evele is with Mina in Neuweier and Mirz is with her carer family in Mannheim) I am dropping you a brief line before I go to bed, because tomorrow, once again I won't be able to write. (...) Pray with me for shalom! My fear is terrible.

Munich, 30 October 1939

Dearest Hilde,
I am trying to think of where to begin this letter to you, after such a long time of enforced silence. God grant that these lines, though they have a long way to travel, may

reach you after all. I am sending them to Hans, my dear, and hope that both he and Liesel have informed you of our whereabouts and our progress. Perhaps you also know about the terrible fears and anxieties that plagued us at the end of August and the beginning of September ... and how suddenly – the entire Kehilla[27] disappeared without even considering – and it's all Greek to me ... poor Sylvia and her two children worth informing. Not to mention that the "parnes"[28] of our community, and all the others didn't even bother to give any thought to what I could do or where we could find shelter. All in the past now, Hilde. One day I was alone with my children in Offenburg with only Dr. Wiegand[29] and Mr. and Mrs Spitzer[30] still there. We had a few horrible weeks during which I tried in vain to join the others with the children. In the meantime, I learned that the rest of the Kehilla had finally been granted shelter here after several unsuccessful attempts elsewhere. After telegraphic back and forth, we put on our long-packed backpacks, took our long-packed suitcases and drove here in a 15-hour eventful night journey. We were immediately given accommodation by the well-organised and friendly local government and our trembling nerves were grateful for so much goodwill. In our first accommodation, four of us lived in one room with 2 beds and 1 divan.

I have almost no asthma here, despite the season. The harsh local climate is good for me. So we had it – very relatively speaking – quite good. After the initial eating out quickly became impossible, I was then allowed to cook very small dishes myself. The children were enrolled in

---

[27] see Note 10
[28] Parnas; "keeper" head of the community
[29] Dr. med. Herta Wiegand (née Lion, 1890–1944 died on transport); practice in Offenburg since 1919
[30] Alexander Spitzer (1867–1941 Gurs) and Helene, née Sternweiler (1887–1963)

the local school, so they liked it very much. Unfortunately, after 4 weeks, we had to leave the first accommodation because the lady of the house herself was forced to move out. Now we live far out in a suburb, in a very fine house in a good neighbourhood. We're on the 5th floor again, but as there is a lift and I have the lift key as well as the house key, it is not too bad this time. At first, living this high was a disaster for me. I had to put Esther up here in the Jewish children's home with the help of the lovely refugee welfare office, after she had made life almost impossible for me …for all of us in our one room …with her tantrums. Now she is doing well – we women always do – and my heart is recovering. Terrible that it should be so. This gives you the broader outline of our life here. I cook, study with the children and because of their long school days, long tram journeys and many chores, I have hardly any time. I often think I cannot continue like this, but at least we have enough to eat, so please don't worry about that, Hilla. I can't and don't want to write much about my mental condition, sister. You know me and you know what this time of being cut off from my husband, from what gives my life meaning, means to me. I suffer – oh, how I suffer. Fortunately, I still receive regular news from Ed (via Liesel and Swiss friends) and I know, if I can believe it, that he is healthy and doing well. He is currently trying to get the children and me to the USA (with an affidavit), but alone, without him. Will he succeed? Oh Hilde, how I dread that too …going to the USA without Ed, but it seems to be the lesser of the two evils. It feels as if we are just puppets whose fate is completely under the control of the whims of the puppeteer. There is so much between heaven and earth that cannot be written about. Despite the ban, many people from here are currently going to Eretz legally, having obtained certificates. I see this and I am filled with bitterness.

Sis, dear, please send me news of Liesel or Hans. How are you? How are you living? Pray for peace soon and for our salvation! Your loving Sylvia

Card from Sylvia Cohn to Dr. Hertha Wiegand, Offenburg 22 October 1940, written at 12 o'clock, postmarked 8 o'clock on the day of her deportation with Eva and Myriam to Gurs (the camp in the South of France). The card shows that the deportees were told they would be taken to Chalon:

Offenburg, 22 October 1940, 12 midnight

My Dear, Good Doctor,
These are my final and most sincere greetings and wishes for you. A thousand thanks! May God in heaven, if he exists, bless you. Stay with your child! I would not go without my children, who are so young and lively. Please take care of my poor little Esther (*Esther was too weak and somewhat disabled from infantile polio to travel*). We hear we are being taken to Chalon. If I can, I will send word.

God bless you, (…). I love you so much, Farewell, mother, Yours Sylvia[31]

---

[31] Offenburg Municipal Archive, fonds 9: Wiegand I/32 estate
30 Eva Mendelsson: Techessakna is a Hebrew song that was sung at the end of most performances

(Card) Sylvia Cohn, Camp de Gurs, Block J, Barrack 16,
9 February 1941

Dear Mr. and Mrs Neu[32],

On behalf of the children of Offenburg, as well as on behalf of my own children, I thank you very much for the bread you sent, which was eaten with joy and gratitude.

Be happy that you are free. The children and I have no chance whatsoever of being released, although thank God, after 14 days, I have at last again received direct news from my husband in England. He is doing his best – but neither he nor I believe he will be successful and he cannot even send us money because of the stringent exchange controls there Otherwise he is doing well, thank God, better than we are. We are constantly being vaccinated and I am just about sick of it and everything else here too. We hear that we will soon be moved to another camp near Perpignan, close to the sea. It is "supposed" to be better there … we'll see. I am very fearful and Uncle Achilles[33] is fading by the day. I don't think he will be able to take it much longer.
Best regards
Yours, Sylvia Cohn

---

[32] Emil and Clementine Neu from Offenburg. Emil Neu was the long-standing community chairman: he too was deported to Gurs with the Offenburg community

[33] Encrypted message due to censorship: There is too little food!

(letter)
Sylvia Cohn, Centre d'hebergés Rivesaltes, P. O. Block B 29

Dear Mr. and Mrs Neu,
Did you receive my card from Gurs a few months ago, in which I thanked you for the bread you were so kind to send to the children?

I wish I were still writing from there. In the meantime, we have come to this camp, which is much more scenic, being about 10–12 km from the sea, and we no longer have barbed wire around us and, with a great deal of imagination, we can imagine that we are free people on our way from one block to another. These are the good points about this location. The giant camp covers an absolutely vast area *(redacted)* and we are living under the same conditions as on the outside, well, no, not really under the same conditions. It is more than a pity that you and many others there and elsewhere cannot visit us *(redacted)*. Just before Passover we were moved to another block, which *(redacted)* was formerly occupied by *(redacted)*.

My letter to you today is an urgent plea for help. My dear Mr. and Neu, please do not turn down my request and send me and my poor children parcels with anything edible that you can find, for full payment and if you give me the amount, I will sen dit to you in advance. *(redacted)*, and I really don't know what to do any more. I have no one to send me anything. My sister, who sent me parcels to Gurs, is not allowed to do so here, because parcels sent from the same Département are forbidden. Besides, they have to move on again tomorrow and leave the Perpignan area, the poor things, with no clue of where they can go.

I often have good news from my dear husband, thank goodness, but my prospects of release and onward migration to the USA are – alas – nil, as a letter from my previous guarantor, which I received the day before yesterday, explained to me that he could no longer renew the affidavits, which had already been extended three times, as he felt old and ill. So I don't even have a guarantor at the moment, which means that we are as good as buried here. My husband is doing his best for us, but he can't get away from where he is during the war, nor can he send me any parcels or money, despite my urgent appeals.

Forgive me for writing this letter, but I really don't know how to help myself here any more, and day after day, I hear the children crying to see Uncle Achilles in such a bad way.

Perhaps you can give me some advice as to what my chances of release are, if I can place the children in a children's home and obtain 800–1000 francs a month from

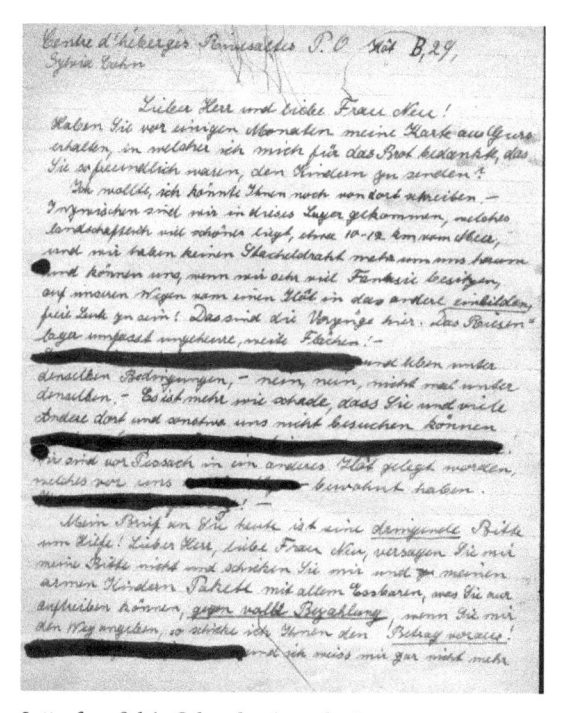

Letter from Sylvia Cohn, showing redactions

America? Up to now, I really haven't wanted to take this course, but if it is at all possible, I would now. All the best to you both, and warm regards from your unhappy Sylvia Cohn.

Sylvia Cohn, Centre d'hebergés Rivesaltes, P. 0. Block B 29, 21 June 1941

Dear Mr. and Mrs Neu,
Your letter was delayed, but it has arrived and I was delighted to read what you have written. However, I was a little disappointed with the parcel, as were all the Offenburg people here, because these are items we can also buy for the same price in the camp. We would have been so happy with certain unbranded foods that are so badly needed. Nevertheless, thank you very much for your effort. Mr Max Weil and Mrs Johanna Cahn asked me to wait a few more days before sending the money. Mr Adolf Kahn is the only one who has already given me his share and Mr Stern wants to send it to you himself. I will send you the money I have received and the amount I owe at the beginning of next week. Thank you very much. I have registered my children for a children's home because their condition makes it urgent. Regrettably, they are still here and I cannot take any steps to procure my own release until they are in the children's home, although unfortuntely, my release remains highly doubtful for other reasons too. My guarantor, who had faithfully and dutifully given an affidavit for 3 years and renewed it again and again, informed me on Erev Pesach that he can no longer renew the surety due to his illness. This has left me in an unenviable situation for the past 8 months and more, without any prospect of a positive change. I often have good news from my husband,

but unfortunately, very seldom from Esther, who is still in Munich. She has left school and is studying languages and business. Oh, my dear Neus, when will the war, this misery, come to an end? Best regards,
Yours, Sylvia Cohn

(Letter)
Sylvia Cohn, Centre d'hébergés Rivesaltes, P. O. Block B 29,
31 July 1941

Dear Family Neu,
I am writing to thank you for your kind letter on the first day I was released from the infirmary after a 3-week stay. It was not my fault, but force majeure prevented the money from reaching you for so long. When I wanted to send it to you many weeks earlier, it was not possible, and when it was possible, the delays had become very extended. I hope that by now, you have received the 105 francs (from me and Mr. Kahn). None of the others paid me as they told me that they would deal with you themselves. It is a pity that you don't believe me, but thank God, you are not experiencing the conditions here yourselves, where we have virtually no money and indeed, not a single France for some time and that is worse than bad, because we have no reserves left.

I was sent to the infirmary because of heart problems, severe dizziness and other such symptoms. The peace and quiet there, a bed and some milk every day did me a lot of good – but it was also necessary. Unfortunately, the children have still not left. This causes me great grief, but I cannot change it. Yesterday Mirzel *(Myriam)* also went to the infirmary in Block J, a half hour walk from here, for some very necessary care and to build up her strength. There, my very tall, thin and anaemic child is now receiving milk and injections to build her up. Evchen is with me, but would really also need the same care and attention.

The best things in my life are the letters which, thank God, often come from London and less frequently from Estherle. My dear husband always wants to comfort and cheer me up, to encourage me to persevere with his wonderful trust in God and his confidence that this war will soon end well. If only I could be so confident.

Esther is attending a Higher Education and Business college in Munich. She still lives in the children's home under thewatchful eye of the Almighty and all the dear friends I made in Munich during our stay are also taking loving care of the child, including my landlords and especially, Dr. Finkelscherer. By the way, the younger Dr. Bruno Finkelscherer is now engaged, and Esther writes that his fiancée is a very nice girl. I have given Estherle the option of spending the long holidays in Offenburg with Uncle Leopold if she wants to. He won't be thrilled with this, but he might be able to take care of a few things for me.

Yes, I believe you when you say that you have worries and cares too. But then again, has any of us ever lived free from worry, even when times were relatively good? Never ... That's how stupid we were. And thank God, dear Mr. and Mrs. Neu, that your dear children took you out of Gurs so quickly. There is no comparison. Hopefully you both have good reports from your dear relatives, good Mutterle in W. (Wangen) and dear Grandpa. Please don't forget us completely and accept warm greetings from your
Sylvia Cohn

I regret to report that Mr. Adolf Kahn[34] is not doing well. He has been ill for 5 weeks, and we fear the worst.

---

[34] Adolf Kahn from Offenburg, Schanzstr. 7 (1880–28.8.1941 Rivesaltes)

Plays

Sylvia Cohn also wrote playlets for various occasions. They were usually performed for the first time at events organised by the Jewish community in the Offenburg synagogue. Two of these plays have survived. They deal with biblical themes: "Ahasuerus [Xerxes]" and "Esther, a Purim play". Ahasuerus was first performed in 1937.

```
                    E s t h e r .
           '- Ein Purimspiel  von Sylvia Cohn-Oberbrunner.

Personen: König Ahasveros,                Gefolge und Mädchen der Königin
          Königin Esther,                 Gefolge des Königs
          Minister Haman                  Mehrere Juden
          Ein Jude, Mordechai,            Herolde
          1.Kammerdiener Charbonah,       2 Verschwörer, Bigdan u. Teresch .
          2. Kammerdiener Mehuman,

          -Ort der Handlung : Am persischen Königshof, Stadt Susa.

                           1. Akt.
1.Scene Charbona, Mehuman, Herold.

Charbona: Sagt, habt Ihr es denn schon vernommen,
          Was im Hause des Königs passiert?
          Königin Vaschti sollte zum König kommern
          Und hat den Befehl  n i c h t  ausgeführt!
Mehuman:  Ein schlechtes Beispiel hat sie gegeben
          Für a l l e Frauen im ganzen Land,
          Nun wird es n i r g e n d s Gehorsam mehr geben,
          Erschüttert wird aller Ehen Bestand.
Charbona: O weh, - was soll daraus nun werden,
          Wenn jede Frau tut, was sie will? -
          Das wär' die Hölle ja auf Erden - -
          Doch - halt - was hör' ich da? sei still -
Herold:   (tritt auf und bläst in die Trompete, allerlei Volk eilt herbei
          und hört zu.)
          Im Namen des Königs hab' ich zu verkünden,
          Verstossen sei Vaschti, die Königin fein,
          Ihr Ungehorsam muss Strafe finden,
          Nun wird eine a n d e r e  Königin sein!
Volk, Bigdan u. Teresch:
          Habt Ihr's gehört? Das geschieht ihr schon recht!
          Die Vaschti passte zur Königin schlecht,
          Nun muss sie gehn, und alle Frauen
          Werden daran ein Beispiel schauen
          Und werden nun nicht mehr, zanken und schrei'n
          Und fürder doppelt so folgsam sein!
Herold:   (bläst in die Trompete)
          Zum zweiten hab' ich zu erzählen,
          Die schönste Jungfrau, die man findit,
          Will sich der König zum Weibe erwählen,
          Herbei nun, Ihr persischen Mädchen, geschwind!
          Schmückt Euch, bekränzt Euch, seid sittig und fein,
          Wer wird die Auserwählte sein?
Herold geht ab.
das Volk: Auf, auf, ihr Mädchen, nun schnell nach Haus,
          Holt eure besten Gewänder heraus,
          Schmückt euch, bekränzt euch, seid sittig und fein,
          Wer wird die Auserwählte sein?
das Volk zerstreut sich und verlässt die Bühne?
```

Ahasuerus [Xerxes].
A play staged in ten images

Ahasuerus, a furrowed, very old, stooped, bearded Jew with the haunted and weary look of the persecuted, staggers onto the stage, dressed in rags and carrying a tall staff. He sits down on a stone at the front of the stage, rests his head on his arm and speaks:

Ahasuerus [Xerxes]:
I am many thousands of years old.
I am weary and burnt out.
Across deserts and oceans and on roads
I have been forced to roam, always running.
Wherever I was, in every land
it has been the same for me.
First, they offered me the hand of friendship,
then they took me prisoner.
Wherever I went, the same suffering.
First they welcomed me,
they gave me a place to live, bread and clothes,
then they took it from me.

For one I was too clever,
and for another, too diligent,
so that many were green with envy,
and to none was I acceptable.
Yes, indeed. Yet, to many a prince,
the Jew's life was highly esteemed.
They liked me as one may like
the juice a lemon gives,

but not the lemon itself.
They left me in peace for a time,
and I earned money by working hard.
Then, these princes, they milked me like a cow
and persecuted me to destruction.
That was all the love I found
on the stony paths I trod.
My eyes, head and hands are stinging.
Where may I lie down?
For thousands of years this staff has been
my most faithful companion, (*takes it in his hand*)
and it will yet accompany me to the grave,
to my eternal rest in the cool of the earth.
Lord God, let there be an end
to the horror of this endless wandering,
and take this aged wandering Jew home.
Let him see your kingdom.
For, Oh Lord God, after this eternity
I long for peace.
I bear the mark of millennia of sorrow
and I am weary, so weary.
(*Ahasuerus falls asleep, resting his hand on his staff*)

Image
A translucent curtain descends and through it, all the events on stage are clearly visible. Three half-naked men are dragging heavy stones. They groan under the load. They hammer and chip at the stones. One of them stops, exhausted. The Egyptian overseer stands with his whip raised, about to beat the exhausted man. From off-stage, the narrator is heard:

Narrator:
Ruinous toil and hard labour
are the legacy from our forefathers.
The whip was the reward of the weary.

Where, where was the saviour?
(The first image remains for a few minutes, then the curtain rises)

Image
Medieval townscape, town square with fountain. A woman is drinking. She drops to the ground, hand on her heart. Dead bodies litter the ground. Two Jews in traditional Galician dress are walking along the pavement. Three horrified women gesticulate and point at them.

Narrator (off-stage):
Thousands of people are dying
With the harvest comes the black death.
From where does such ruin come?
Who is to blame for this plague?
Monks, priests, radical Catholic flagellants,
with their speeches of dark intent
are inciting the people
against the Jews.
(*curtain*)

Image
The same place. On stage is a stake built high. The crowd is excitedly signalling and gesticulating as the people await the spectacle of the burning.

Narrator (off-stage)
Since the Middle Ages
they have been blamed for everything.
They lament their wretched fate.
They are cruelly murdered.
Woeful cries resound
and gruesome moaning is heard
as the flames crackle, every day anew.

The blaze from the pyres stacked high
drifts upwards to the heavens.
Thousands of the wretched
are executed every day with
a thousand seeking death themselves
and in those times the rabble
rejoiced in pious frenzy
and enjoyed watching the grisly spectacle
which they said was pleasing to God.
(curtain)

Image
A poorly furnished parlour. Wooden chairs, a table. Old, dignified Jew in traditional dress, with long white beard and skullcap, bent over a thick book. Around him, a group of students listen intently.

Narrator:
To serve God in another way
was the path of our pious forefathers.
To make atonement by giving
although life was meagre and hard.
Even if the rabble pour out their vitriol
and life hangs but by a hair,
close your eyes and let us pray
for those who were, are and will be
ready to die for the cause and
let us immerse ourselves
in the wellspring of our holy scriptures,
as we seek to learn, teach and give.
They died without complaint whose fate it was,
with spiritual banners flying high and
holding aloft the shield of Torah.
Yes, they were our forefathers
as if wrapped in armour

and despite all the hatred, scorn and jealousy
they remained true to the teachings.
Hunger only fuelling the zeal.
Hunger liberating the soul.
Intoxicated, reflecting on their life
as they turned over the pages
of the book of life,
God's nearness making them tremble,
replete as they were with God's teachings.
(curtain)

Image
A magnificently dressed prince, his cloak casually draped around his shoulders, hands a scroll of parchment to a Jew bowing and kartowing before him. The Jew, on the other hand, gives the prince a thick leather pouch full of gold.

Narrator:
'Isaac', smiles the Serene Highness,
'You have given me gold:
you can count on me when you need it.
I'll protect you.'

Image
Ghetto walls, behind the locked wrought iron gate, Jewish children, stretching out their skinny arms through the iron bars. Children with hungry eyes. In front, a medieval mercenary soldie stamps up and down

Narrator:
Blue skies, golden sunshine,
meadows in spring colours
where happy children play
with hoops and bows and arrows.
Alas, our children did not know

the joys those children knew.
The law and harsh conditions
kept them locked into skid row.

Image
Another time. A young man is standing on a gallery, his eyes shining, he is holding a roll of parchment, others are gesticulating. A crowd of male and female workers look up and listen, fascinated.

Narrator:
Late freedom struck their hearts.
Sunlight after the black night,
and from the bitter pain of servitude
they awoke, overjoyed too soon.
Freedom at last took them
to the highest heights.
Those who have cast off their chains
also want to see their brothers set free.

Picture
A few students in traditional German fraternity dress parade through the streets. Overdressed ladies in heavy make up and fur coast with lapdogs are watching the young students.

Narrator:
Doctor this, doctor that,
Mr. Lawyer, Mr. Commissioner,
my son, the city architect,
well, we have great expectations for him
'My son's a teacher – 'mine's a doctor',
Notary Public Meier, Judge Cohn and all that
It was a time of heady excitement,
being free at last,
free to climb the ladder of life,

higher and higher, further and further.
It wasn't arrogance, no, it was simply the old longing
to make life easier for the children.
and at any cost to preserve the children
from the bitter burden endured by the parents.

Image
In front of the pillar bearing the notice of the Nuremberg Laws. Groups of frightened Jewish men on the right, frightened Jewish women on the left.

Narrator:
And people stare at the pillar ...
Surely it can't be true, it must be a hoax?
There is sun, freedom, knowledge and light ...
But only for the others. Not for us.
The old curse descends,
the perpetual wandering Jews.
People without a land. People for the grave.

Image
Landscape in Erez Israel. Shadowing mountains in the background. Pioneers at work picking oranges. They sing the Emek – Song of the Valley describing the Israeli landscape. Ahasuerus [Xerxes] awakes, looks around in amazement and speaks:

Ahasuerus [Xerxes].
What is this new spirit
that points the way here?
Am I still dreaming? Or has it really been
translated from dream to real life?
What is this new generation
that, if my eyes do not deceive me,
wield their hoes and spades with pride
and feel joy in their work?

Their eyes shine ... they are singing!
Despite the hard work, the mood is cheerful,
their faces tanned, their bodies toned.
Only a holy miracle could have done this.
That my old eyes can still bear witness to it
and see our people rebuilding our land,
the old home, bride of the heart,
the landscape so strangely familiar to the soul
My God, how far we have travelled!
The clothes I wore along the way
have long since crumbled into dust.
My God, how hard was the path.
How often did I cry: I CANNOT GO ON.
Oh Lord, how agonising was the way.
Now I may rest, happy in the knowledge
that our faithful mother earth, the Holy Land,
will take her weary son by the hand
and give him what no one ever gave him:
a peaceful grave in the earth of our Eretz.
My God Almight, thank you.

Ahasuerus [Xerxes] collapses and dies, a smile on his lips. The chanting of the pioneers swells, they sing the Tekessaknah – a Hebrew song sung at the end of most Jewish events.
(curtain)

ESTHER
A biblical Purim[35] play by Sylvia Cohn

Characters:
King Ahasuerus[Xerxes].
Queen Esther
Haman, Prime Minister
Mordechai, a Jew
Charbona, a servant
Mehuman, a servant
Queen's retinue and maids
King's retinue
Several Jews
Heralds
Bigtan and Teresh, conspirators
Place: The Persian royal court

Act 1
Scene 1
(Charbona, Mehuman, Herald enter)

Charbona: Tell me, have you heard what's happening at the king's palace? Queen Vashti was commanded to come to the King and she's refused.
Mehuman: Well, she's set all the women in the land a pretty bad example. Now the women every-

---

[35] Probably created in spring 1935 as a contribution to a competition organised by the Jewish Cultural Association; cf. footnote [1]

where will stop doing what they're told and every marriage is likely to suffer.

Charbona: Oh dear, what will become of us now if every woman does what she wants. It'd be hell on earth! But hang on, what's this I hear? Shhh.. Be quiet!

Herald: *(steps up and blows the trumpet, the crowd hurries over to listen)*

In the name of the King I hereby proclaim that the King has repudiated Queen Vashti and sent her away in disgrace. Her disobedience must be punished and the King will choose another to be his queen.

Crowd, servants: Have you heard? It serves her right! Vashti wasn't right for the job anyway. Now she's been sent away in disgrace, women will see what can happen if they are disobedient and they will probably stop their nagging and be twice as obedient!

Herald: (*blows trumpet*) Moreover, good subjects, the King will choose for his wife the fairest maiden in the land. Come along, ladies of Persia, dress up in all your finery and put on your make up, be modest and attractive to have a chance of being chosen.

(Herald leaves)

Crowd: Come on girls, hurry home and dress in your finest clothes, put on your make up and go join the line up. We wonder who the King will choose?

(The crowd disperses and leaves the stage. Enter slowly)

Scene 2
Mordechai and Esther

Mordechai: The time has come to let go my foster child. Esther, my dear, I brought you up in discipline and piety. Now don't forget me, promise me you won't forget me. I give you my blessing, my child, remember to be obedient, faithful and good, but if the King should take a fancy to you, perhaps you might keep quiet about having Jewish blood.

Esther: I'm so nervous, my heart is beating really fast. Farewell, dear Uncle, and a thousand thanks.

(Esther enters the King's palace. Mordechai remains standing in the shadows in the wings, pondering. Well-dressed girls hurry into the palace from all sides).

Scene 3
(Enter two hooded figures wearing black masks, Bigtan and Teresh, conspirators)

Bigtan: (*quietly*) Well? When are going to do it? I don't wanna be a servant here any longer. But we must hop it fast when the deed is done. You've got to do it with me. I don't dare do it alone.

Teresh: Oh, shut up! We don't want Ahasuerus hearing about our plan before we can finish him off. He would do for us and there'd be nobody out there to help us.

(Conspirators leave the stage).

Mordechai: See what these villains are plotting? The King's murder! Ahasuerus won't be suspecting a thing. I must get word to him and warn him.

(He calls Charbona and whispers to him)

Act 2
Scene 1

(*A crowd is milling around in front of the palace. Mordechai is there too. Two heralds, and later Haman, enter. Two heralds cross the stage, leading away the conspirators in chains*)

The crowd: Did you see that? That's what happens if you plot to assassinate the King. Now they're going to have to pay for their crime. Treason must be punished.

(*Enter Haman. Everyone bows low, except Mordechai who remains standing*)

Haman: Who is the dog that does not bow down before the King's Prime Minister like everyone else? He's a Jew, I can see it in his face. The rogue shall pay for this, I swear: I'll make him sorry for his arrogance ... and not just him ... he's to blame for the rest of his people suffering the same fate.

(*The people disperse. curtain*)

Scene 2
(*Enter the King, Haman*)

King: Ah, Haman, what brings you to see me? Do I detect a touch of resentment in your expression? Has anyone here annoyed you? If they have, I'll banish them from court.

Haman: (*craftily*) It's no-one in particular, honoured King, who has upset me so much. No, just one wouldn't bother me. It's an entire people who have made me so angry. They live here, in your kingdom, but by their own rules, laws and customs. They worship their own god and that seems a bit of an insult to your dignity. They are arrogant, insolent and proud. They're a thoroughly rotten lot.

King: Well, let's not hang around: take action now! Here's my seal and with it, they will know how powerful I am in this country. Do with them as you wish. I give them to you with all their assets. After all, anyone who lives in my kingdom must serve me, for I am Persia and Persia is me. Send out messengers to let the public know what's happening.

(exit the King)

Haman: *(mutters to himself)* The King is putty in my hands! How quickly I've got what I wanted. Now Mordechai will see what his arrogance has done and I will rejoice as the Jew trembles and pales. I'll do what's necessary. We'll cast lots to choose the day of the bloodbath. These Jews are weak and easily conquered. Their money will fall into our laps. That Mordechai is the worst of the lot. I can't wait to hang him on the gallows.

(leaves the stage)
(curtain)

Act 3

Scene 1

(heralds, a crowd on stage, then enter complaining Jews)

Herald 1: I bring news, people. Oh joy unbounded! You may dance and sing and celebrate for Esther, the new Queen, is as beautiful as the roses that bloom in the morning dew.

Chorus, girls and crowd: Long live Queen Esther! We are devoted and loyal to her and pray that our sister's good fortune will be ours too.

Scene 2
(Girls dance in a circle. The Queen appears in all her finery, the girls dance around her as music plays)

Scene 3
(Two heralds, the crowd, Jews. Trumpet blast, the girls and the Queen scurry away into the palace)

2nd Herald: In the name of the King, I proclaim the following, so hear these words: all Jews shall perish. Henceforth, no Jew shall live on Persian soil. Anyone who manages to stab or strangle a Jew to death shall have the King's thanks. Let them all be despatched on the same day and I hereby declare that day is the thirteenth of Adar.

Some of the people:
Did you hear? Did you hear? Mordechai's pride has done for him! Now here's a fine thing, there'll be lots of loot for us ... Ha, what's the value of a Jew's life? There'll be plenty of gold and silver.

Others: Oh really? Is that what you think? It won't be for us, that horrible Haman will take it all.

(exit heralds and crowd)

Scene 4
(Jews come from all sides, looking defeated, bent over double, first Mordechai enters in sackcloth. A guard stands in front of the palace)

Chorus of Jews: Help, save us! Hear our cries. What can we do? We need help! Let us fast and pray. All of us have been condemned to death.

Mordechai: God in heaven, hear our prayer and look upon your people, Israel, your children, how they trample us underfoot ... and only because we are Jews.

Chorus of Jews: Help, save us, hear our weeping, hear our prayers, Oh God, the Almighty, the One, may you not be deaf to our pleas.

Mordechai: Let us pray, raise our hands in supplication. Our God is a good and merciful God ... (*pause and prayer*) but all the same, I will send word to Esther, that she may save us from our fate.

(*Mordechai whispers to the servant Charbona*)

Chorus of Jews: Help, save us, hear our cries. Almighty God, hear our distress. You alone can set us free, Haman is sending us all to our death.

(*curtain*)

Act 4
Scene 1
(*Bedchamber of the King. On stage are the King and his valet Charbona, later Haman enters*).

King: I lie awake hour after hour until the sleepless night ends and morning comes. Oh dear, what can I do to pass the time? I know! I'll read the chronicles of our history.

King: *(calling out)* Charbona!

Charbona: Your Majesty?

King: Tell me, my boy, can you read? Go quickly and bring me the big book that chronicles our history and you shall read it to me and I will discover everything that's taken place.

Charbona: As the King commands.

(Goes away and comes back with a thick book, sits down at Ahasuerus' feet)

Charbona: *(reads)*: "It happened in the third year of your reign, Your Majesty, that a Jew, Mordechai, saved you from death. He overheard two conspirators planning to murder you and so he quickly sent word to the Queen, and it was she who saved the day and the plan was foiled." That's what it says here in your chronicle.

King: I've never heard that before. This is the first I know of it. What did the man get for having saved the King's life? I want him to be right royally honoured!

Charbona: Mordechai got nothing, Sire, well ... he's only a Jew, poor wretch.

King: Call Haman!

Charbona: Haman, come in!

Haman: This can only mean one thing. No doubt
(to himself) about it and I'll tell him what he wants to hear.

(Turning to the King:)

To such a man, Oh Majesty, who is so much in your favour, I would accord the highest honour. I would wrap him in your own fine cloak, buckle your own sword on him, mount him on your own horse and the highest and most noble man in the land shall lead him through the streets and proclaim for all to hear: 'This is how the King honours the man who deserves his thanks!'

King: Your advice is good, I see it now. You are the highest noble in the land. Now do everything you have suggested to Mordechai, who saved me from assassination.

Haman: (*an angry aside*) Oh curses and damnation, that I should have to do all that? And give this Jew the honour! Well, I'd never have guessed ... and now everyone will laugh at me. I'm incandescent with rage and yet ... and yet ... I must carry out the command.

(*curtain*)

Act 5

Scene 1

(*Queen Esther's quarters. Esther, her handmaids, the valet Charbona*)

Esther: What is all this weeping and wailing I've been hearing at court for many days now? Isn't that Mordechai I can see outside? Oh dear, my heart is touched by a strange foreboding ...

Charbona: Madam, he sends me to you with sad tidings. You must go urgently to the King and beg him to stop wicked Haman from having all the Jewish people slaughtered.

Esther: Oh, how dreadful! I am absolutely horrified. But how can I help the situation? I'm forbidden from going to see the King in his quarters unless he sends for me and if I don't obey the rule, I could be put to death myself.

Charbona: But Mordechai is begging you urgently. You must take the risk. Surely you've heard all the weeping and wailing: I don't know how you can sleep.

Esther: I heard it, I heard it, but I refused to listen. Now I am heartsick with grief and I will go and ask the King to see me, even if it means losing my life.

(Charbona leaves. Esther puts on a lovely outfit and immaculate make up, goes into the forecourt and waits)

Scene 2
(The King arrives, sees Esther standing there humbly, hands her the sceptre as a sign of his favour)

King: What's the matter, dearest Esther, my Queen? What is it that brings you here to me? I am so fond of you, ask me anything you like and I shall grant your every wish.

Esther: Beloved King and husband, grant me the honour of coming to a feast I am preparing.. and please bring Haman too. I came here to invite you in person.

King: Well, if that's all, my dear child, certainly, yes – we'll come.

(King leaves)

Scene 3
(Esther and her servants are setting the table)

Esther *(praying)* Oh Lord, did you lift me up far above my sisters in Israel for the purpose of pleading for my people at this hour of need? Yes, my people Israel are in dire straits, and I am weak. Oh Lord, giver of life and death, bless my purpose. I'm still young and have a life to live and I've been fearful and trembling. But that's past now, so forgive me and give me the courage to do whatever it takes to save my people.

Heavenly Father, grant me the grace to do it today.

(enter the King and Haman)

Scene 4
(*Esther, King, Haman, Charbona sit at a table laid with food and wine*)

King: Esther, loveliest of all women, Let me look into your eyes. Your feast is well prepared. Everything is delicious, and the wine is especially well chosen. Ask me whatever you want and I will grant your wish.

Esther: Ah, my beloved Lord and King, I am only an unimportant woman and yet you are so good to me. Deliver me from evil and be merciful to my people and save them from perishing. Because, you see, we've been betrayed. An evil enemy is set on killing us all.

King: What? Who is this and where is he? Bring me the villain and I'll make him pay.

Haman: (*prostrating himself, whimpering*) Mercy, mercy!

Esther: He lies at your feet. Haman is the villain: look how his face grows pale. It was Haman, knowing he was in your favour, who devised the plot to hang Mordechai on the gallows. Indeed, he's already built the gallows.

King: He'd do that without asking me, would he? He'll wish he hadn't. Now I am deaf to his pleading. Let him be hanged from those self same gallows.

(*Two servants hurry and lead Haman away*)

Esther: Now a millstone has dropped from my heart. My king is just and good, but this still causes me much pain when I think of all the poor, innocent Jews. The command has gone out to kill them all on the same day. I would gladly sacrifice myself to save them.

King: Now calm your poor heart, my dear, and I will see to it. Herald!

Herald: What is your command, Sire?

King: Go quickly and spread the new message far and wide. Let the Jews throughout the land take up arms for their own protection. Then, no-one will dare to touch them. Be happy, my dearest, because your Jews are saved.

Chorus: Now Haman must pay for his crimes, for his soul is an evil one. Now he is the tormented one. Ours is a just God.

(*King leaves. Esther mid-stage, Jews crowd in from all sides*)

Chorus of Jews: Let us rejoice and sing praises. Put away your sackcloth and ashes and let us praise the Lord God for His miracle of setting us free.

End

Bibliography

Literature on the history of the Offenburg Jews

Flügler, Ursula: ...was sich alles anknüpft an die Gräber [What the graves can tell us]. In: Manfred Bosch (ed.), Alemannisches Judentum. Traces of a Lost Culture. Eggingen 2001, 528–531. – Dies. (ed.): Jüdischer Friedhof Offenburg. Poems. Literature course 1986/87. Okengymnasium Offenburg, 1987

Germania Judaica. Vol. II: From 1238 to the middle of the 14th century. Ed. by Zvi Avneri. Tübingen, 1968

Hundsnurscher, Franz – Taddey, Gerhard: Die jüdischen Gemeinden in Baden-Württemberg. Stuttgart, 1988 [History of the Jewish communities of B-W]

Kähni, Otto: History of the Offenburg Jewish Community. In: The Ortenau 49 (1969), 80–114

Lewin, Adolf: Geschichte der badischen Juden seit der Regierung Karl Friedrichs (1738–1909). Karlsruhe, 1909 [History of the Jewish communities of B-W under the government of Elector Karl Friedrich]

Möschle, S.: The Fate of the Jewish Population of Offenburg under the National Socialists. Graduate dissertation for the teaching profession. University of Freiburg, 1977

Rosenthal, Berthold: Heimatgeschichte der badischen Juden seit ihrem geschichtlichen Auftreten bis zur Gegenwart. [History of the Jews of Baden since they were first there up to the present] Bühl, 1927 (reprint Magstadt, 1981)

Ruch, Martin: Three Jewish Libraries in the Ortenau (Offenburg, Kippenheim, Lahr). In: The Ortenau 83 (2003), 77–82

Idem: "I ask for a few more stars" – Jewish voices from Offenburg, vol. 2. Offenburg, 2002

Idem: The Offenburg artist Oscar Haberer (1867–1932): "Prototype of the best that lives in the Jewish soul ...". In: The Ortenau 82 (2002)

Idem: The "Salmen". History of the Offenburg Synagogue. Offenburg, 2002

Idem: Sources on the history of the Offenburg Jews in the 17th century. E-publication, University Library Freiburg (Freidok), 2001

Idem: Pictures of the deportation of the Baden-Palatinate Jews to Gurs. In: The Ortenau 80 (2000), 253–260

Idem: The last Rabbi of Offenburg. In memoriam Bernhard Gries (1917–1938). In: The Ortenau 80 (2000), 261–268

Idem: The good place. Jewish cemetery Offenburg, documentation of graves (with Samuel Dzialoszynski). Offenburg, 2000

Idem: Jewish Offenburg. A tour. Haigerloch, 1999

Idem: Chased out of the homeland. On the history of the Neu family. The fate of the Jews from Offenburg and South Baden. Constance, 1998

Idem: Forever on the move. The life of Siegfried Schnurmann. Jewish Fates from Offenburg and South Baden. Constance, 1997

Idem: Judaica of the Museum im Ritterhaus, Offenburg. Catalogue. Offenburg, 1997

Idem: Persecution and Resistance in Offenburg 1933–1945. Offenburg, 1995

Idem: Jewish voices from Offenburg. Interviews, autobiographical testimonies, written sources on the history of Offenburg Jews in the period 1933–1945. Appendix: Memorial book. Offenburg, 1995

Idem: Family Cohn. Diaries, letters, poems of a Jewish family from Offenburg. Offenburg, 1992

Idem: Dance hall, revolutionary pub, synagogue, warehouse. The history of the "Salmen" in Offenburg. In: The Ortenau 67 (1987), 371–389

Sauer, Paul: Documents on the Persecution of Jewish Citizens in Baden-Württemberg under the National Socialists 1933–1945. Stuttgart, 1966

Sauer, Paul: The Fates of the Jewish Citizens of Baden-Württemberg under the National Socialists 1933–1945. Stuttgart, 1968

Schellinger, Uwe: Fascinosum, Filou and Object of Research: The Amazing Life of the Clairvoyant Ludwig Kahn from Offenburg (1873–ca. 1966). In: The Ortenau 82 (2002), 429–468

Schwanke, Irmgard: Nachbarschaft auf Zeit. Jews and Christians in the Imperial City of Offenburg in the 17th Century. In: Häberlein/ Zürn (eds.): Minorities, Authority and Society in the Early Modern Period. St. Katharinen 2001, 293–316

Stein, Peter: Ein Schiddusch – eine jüdische Ehevermittlung (Arranged marriages in Judaism) in Offenburg 1878. in: Die Ortenau 82 (2002), 469–486

Walter, Kasimir: Das Judenbad in Offenburg. [The Jewish swimming baths in Offenburg] Offenburg, o.J.